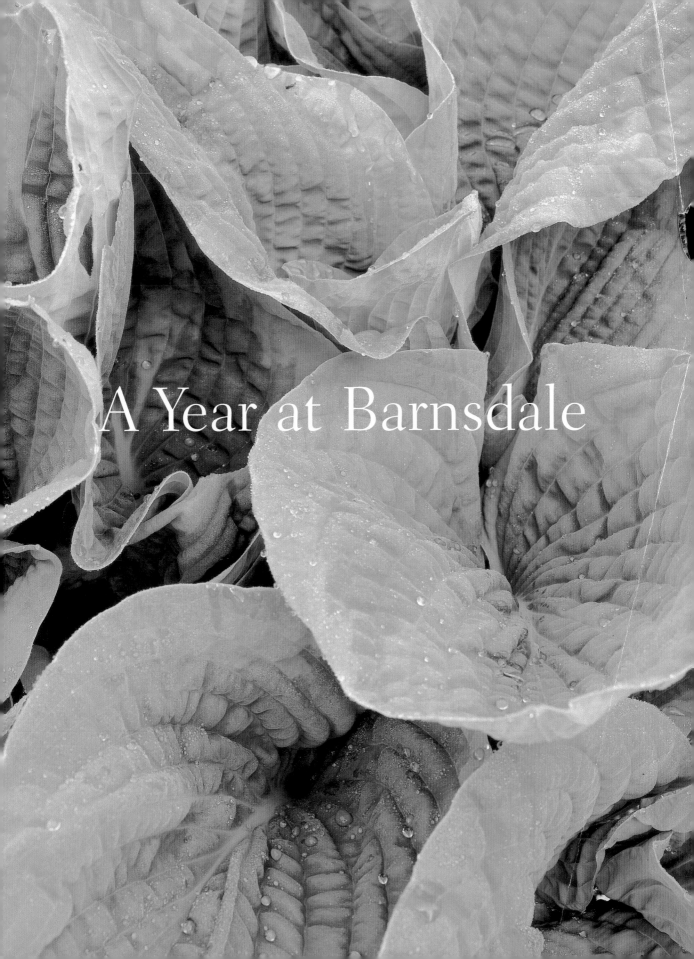

A Year at Barnsdale

Also by Tony Hamilton
Geoff Hamilton's Year in Your Garden
My Brother Geoff

A Year at Barnsdale

The Inspiring Legacy of Geoff Hamilton's Beautiful Garden

Tony Hamilton

headline

First published in 2002
by HEADLINE BOOK PUBLISHING

Tony Hamilton would be happy to hear from
readers with their comments on the book at the
following e-mail address: tony@pta.teamtalk.net

10 9 8 7 6 5 4 3 2 1

Cataloguing in Publication Data is available from
the British Library

ISBN 0 7472 3286 5

Typeset by Letterpart Limited
Set in Fairfield
Designed by Carl Hodson

Printed and bound in France by Pollina n° L86769

HEADLINE BOOK PUBLISHING
A division of Hodder Headline
338 Euston Road
London NW1 3BH
www.headline.co.uk
www.hodderheadline.com

Contents

Introduction

Since Geoff died, in 1996, I have been asked on countless occasions about the future of Barnsdale, his home and the site of his beautiful gardens, from which he presented *Gardeners' World*. It was partly to answer this question that I wrote this book – and partly to explain to his many, many constant devotees what goes on behind the scenes at Barnsdale after Geoff.

Geoff left the gardens and the nursery to his middle son Nick, who is the only one of his three boys to have had a horticultural training and who, at the time of Geoff's death, was running the small nursery close to the gardens. The gardens are now open to the public, with each of the television gardens being maintained as closely to Geoff's design and planting plans as possible, while new gardens are added continuously.

The other two boys, Stephen, the eldest, and Chris, the youngest, each have a share in the profits and Steve, a professional garden photographer, participates by taking all the photographs for the many items of publicity that form a crucial part of Barnsdale's marketing campaigns. He also shot all the photographs that appear in this book. Chris, a teacher and potter, makes exquisite pots for sale in the nursery.

On 15 August 1998 Nick married Sue, who had once been Geoff's secretary. The date was considered to be very auspicious because 15 August was the date of Geoff's birth and also the date on which Sue started work for Geoff fifteen years earlier. When she was recruited to work as Geoff's secretary she had had no horticultural experience, albeit that she was a farmer's daughter, but part of her job description said that when she had no pressing secretarial work to do she should work in the gardens. In fact she enjoyed the gardening more than the secretarial work and before very long she had built a considerable body of knowledge and expertise. Now Nick and Sue are able to work as equal partners in the business, each contributing their bit both in horticultural and business terms.

Nick and Sue, who own and run the gardens, stand proudly among the flowers grown for cutting

The early days after Geoff's death were very hard indeed, because the gardens were originally designed purely as a vehicle for Geoff's work on *Gardeners' World*. This meant that Geoff had been obliged to neglect some parts of the garden from time to time and all the efforts of his very small staff had been concentrated on those parts that were to be used by the BBC in the near future. So it was necessary to get it all into the kind of shape that a visiting garden-lover would expect to see, which was a large and expensive task. Where there was mud there had to be clean, dry paths; where there were overgrown shrubs or intensive weed growth there had to be order and beauty; where there was no access for the disabled this had to be provided. In addition, toilets had to be built, car parks prepared, signs made, leaflets printed, advertising placed – the list of work to be done seemed to go on and on. And it all had to be done with no money, because although Geoff had left Nick the gardens he had left no money to run them. So the bank manager figured large in the planning in the early days.

All these problems were overcome with dogged determination and a lot of hard work and eventually, on 1 March 1997, the gates were opened and the visitors began to arrive. First they came as a dispiriting trickle, but this quickly grew into a torrent and since then the visitor numbers have averaged around 60,000 a year. Five years later, while the bank manager still plays a part in the financial planning, he loses little sleep over the future of Barnsdale: it is clearly no longer at risk. Indeed, the number of visitors now has to be controlled for fear of spoiling the tranquillity of the gardens and reducing the pleasure that the visitors undoubtedly derive from their day – as attested by the glowing comments that fill the visitors' book.

For those who don't already know, I am Geoff's identical twin brother. We had a very close and supportive relationship and I derive great consolation from remembering him and renewing what we had together. What better way to do so than to visit Barnsdale on a frequent basis and to stroll round the beautiful gardens that he created. I used to give Geoff the benefit of my invaluable horticultural advice, which he usually received with a knowing

ABOVE **The bronze bust of Geoff, expertly crafted by his youngest son Chris, is a loving tribute to his father and stands as the centrepiece of the Memorial Garden** RIGHT **Visitors stroll happily through the tranquil and radiant gardens**

grin – because, although I always claimed to have a better garden than he did, we both knew this to be an exaggeration of the worst kind. But then, if you can't insult your own twin brother, who can you insult? Visiting Barnsdale also gives me the occasional opportunity to drink tea with my best friend Lynda, Geoff's wife and soul-mate, who lives in Barnsdale farmhouse, adjacent to but now separated off from the gardens.

Although I visit Barnsdale, I don't give my advice to Nick and Sue. I wisely keep my counsel; and in any case the gardens are a testament to their skill and knowledge. But if I see so much as a blade of grass out of place I make sure that I am seen shaking my head in a posture of despair. I am convinced that such gestures are entirely ignored by the boss, but making them revives some of the satisfaction I used to get by doing the same with Geoff.

By visiting Barnsdale I am able to observe the gardens as they change through the seasons and all that goes on there. What I have tried to provide here is not a gardening book but a simple snapshot of the gardens: the work that goes on in them over a year and the way in which they now offer a memory of Geoff and a learning experience – as well as a huge amount of pleasure – for those who visit them. I hope too that it shows a little of the magnificence of what he created, for I think that the Barnsdale gardens are a testament to his brilliance as a gardener who will rank among the best ever.

ze bust by
ris Hamilton

CHAPTER ONE

~

Work, Wet and Worry

~

January to March

Work, Wet and Worry

~ *January to March*

The trouble with running a garden like Barnsdale – or, for that matter, running any other visitor attraction, whether it be Longleat or Pontins – is that on 1 March visitors will pour through the gates and the place has to be ready to receive them. Not only that but it has to look as though all the running repairs that have had to be done have just happened, as though God waved his hand and resolved all the end-of-season problems, so that visitors will find it better and more enjoyable than they did last year. There must be no sign of the dirt and the disasters that occurred during the sprucing-up operation, of the frayed tempers that may have reared their ugly heads or of the horticultural failures that had to be rectified. Everybody must be smiling and helpful, the lawns must be pristine, the borders colourful and gay, the vegetable gardens cultivated, sown and planted, the coffee hot in the pot and all well in the world.

Nick and Sue plan all that is to happen at Barnsdale with meticulous care during the long, dark winter evenings – preparing work schedules, dreaming up ideas for new gardens, planning exhibits at shows and working out how best to improve and expand the business. Nick says that he is occasionally woken at three o'clock in the morning by Sue saying, 'Hey, Nick, how about this for an idea?' He grudgingly listens and, as politely as he can in such circumstances, suggests they discuss it in the morning. But however thoroughly they plan they, like everybody else working in the great outdoors, have to contend with whatever God and Michael Fish have to throw at them in the form of weather. During the early months of the year 2001, it could hardly have been worse.

January brings the snow – or so they say. But not this year. What January brought this year was rain, rain and more rain. It varied from dramatic, silver, slanting rods to slow, spirit-lowering drizzle, through which the staff at Barnsdale hurried from job to job with mud up to their ears and damp cold piercing through to their bones.

Nick, who trained for three years at Writtle College, Geoff's Alma Mater, and who has some twenty years of experience, has learned that what you can't change you don't worry about. Though she had no formal training, Sue garnered considerable knowledge through

ABOVE LEFT *Corylus avellana* 'Contorta', sometimes known as 'Harry Lauder's Walking Stick' for its curiously twisted shoots, began life as an insignificant specimen when Geoff first established the gardens and has now grown to be a majestic shrub, particularly dramatic when clothed in frost
BELOW The savoy cabbage is decorative at any time, but particularly so when sporting a veil of frost

working at Barnsdale and, through diligent observation, a remarkable memory for plant names and planting conditions coupled with an innate flair for design, she has established herself as a lynchpin in the management team; like Boadicea, she drives her chariot through problems, knife blades flashing, clearly determined to succeed. Nick and Sue both remained surprisingly undaunted by the apparent impossibility of getting everything done, confident that, on the due date, all would be ready.

~

Their confidence was in part due to the fact that they knew they had an excellent team to rely upon. All the ornamental gardening work at Barnsdale is done by a staff of seven, reinforced in the spring and summer by casual labour who carry out the basic but vital tasks of weeding, cleaning and generally keeping the gardens tidy.

There is a head gardener, who at the beginning of 2001 was Gavin Charter. He had been at Barnsdale for about two and a half years, but early in the year he decided that his future lay in garden-centre management and gave notice that he might shortly leave – which would be a blow for Barnsdale.

If Gavin left, it might be a golden opportunity for Jon Brocklebank, the assistant head gardener, working under Gavin. Jon lives at Burton Lazars, near Melton Mowbray, so called because it was once the site of a leper colony. I can vouch for the fact, however, that Jon carries no bell and looks only slightly unclean, mainly around the fingernails. He came to Barnsdale in March 1995 from school, with quite a few GCSEs but no horticultural qualifications. But he was a big, strong lad with lots of potential, so Nick sent him to Brooksby, the local agricultural college, where he qualified in Amenity Horticulture and Landscaping. Jon is particularly comfortable with the visitors; he is also good at plant recognition and botanical names, which is important because, despite the fact that the vast majority of plants are labelled, the question most frequently asked by visitors is: 'What's that plant?'

Alice Marshall is another Brooksby student, who now, having completed the first part of the course at the college

Jon enjoys his conversations with the visitors, most of whom are eager to pick his brains

studying Basic Horticulture, works full time at Barnsdale on a Youth Training Scheme. She toils in the gardens and then has to toil at her books because each week a tutor from Brooksby comes to inspect and discuss her work. They sit in the coffee shop while Alice receives the benefit of the mighty weight of Brooksby know-how and, perhaps, the occasional slap on the wrist for youthful departures from the straight and narrow. She was taken under the warm embrace of Sue's ample wing and, with understanding and good advice, soon began to make rapid progress.

The garden supervisor is Betty Bradley. She has worked at Barnsdale since 1995, so she is one of the people who knew Geoff well and she still speaks warmly of him. When Geoff died, Nick, with no money and an uncertain future, was obliged to lay her off, but he was delighted to be able to welcome her back about a year later, when the business had begun to gather pace. Betty is a dab hand with flower arrangements, so she beautifies every table in the coffee shop with a display of Barnsdale flowers as well as decorating the shop and anywhere else she can lay her hands on. But her main job is in the garden. She is totally unqualified but has a natural talent and bucketsful of enthusiasm, which Nick and Sue value higher than any letters after a name.

Susie Smith (lovely name) came originally to work for three days in the shop but then decided that she'd prefer to work in the gardens. So, with careful though unobtrusive supervision, she took up a job as a gardener and immediately took to it like a duck to water, not only loving the work but also appearing to have caught Betty's most highly prized attribute, contagious enthusiasm. Susie worked only three days a week because she has, quietly grazing the fields around her home, a flock of sheep which she hopes to build up to a sizeable number. She is a trained shepherd with an innate love of the land, which she brought to Barnsdale. At one time in her life she worked with young offenders and during this time developed an enormous patience and understanding, which in turn gave her the ability to deal skilfully with the visitors. That is not, of course, to compare Barnsdale's visitors with young offenders, but it does mean that in Susie they had a friendly, cheerful person to help them with their innumerable queries and occasional needs.

Paul Stacey is a lively, intelligent young man who studied at Writtle College and for his 'sandwich' year, in 2001, in which he had to gain practical experience, worked half at Barnsdale and half with Adam Frost, the brilliant landscape designer who worked for many years at Barnsdale with Geoff and now works independently. Paul has ambitions to get into landscape and garden design and judging by the enthusiasm and energy he displayed at Barnsdale I think he's going to make it. He has also been blessed with the charm and good humour necessary to succeed in business and, apart from the fact that he's young, good-looking, well built and intelligent, all qualities I find intensely irritating, I like him a lot. Remember his name. I have a feeling you'll be hearing a lot more of it in the future.

Oliver Hitchcox, another Brooksby student, comes to Barnsdale for one day a week. He was originally employed because his parents wrote enquiring about a job because the young man suffered from speech difficulties. He's a hugely likeable lad who from the moment he came to Barnsdale never stopped talking. He talks to the staff, to the visitors, to the birds and the bees, to the flowers – anybody or anything that will listen to him. So where the myth of his speech difficulty arose nobody can fathom. Perhaps his parents are cleverer than Nick and Sue realised and inveigled him into the job interview under a cloak of social need – or more plausible is the fact that he is a determined young man and, recognising that he had a difficulty, set about overcoming it with tenacity and great courage. He did well at college, racing through his first examinations and achieving an award for the best performance of his year. Now he has moved on to a more advanced course, which is why he works only one day a week at Barnsdale. However, he is on the weekend rota and during his summer holidays he works right through. It's a great thing to have a few really poor, hungry students about, who are prepared to give their all.

Early in the year a newcomer joined the ranks at Barnsdale – Ben Claridge, a young man who had just finished a horticulture course at Brooksby College. He was employed for a three-month trial period, so started off getting all the dogsbody jobs, poor lad.

It had become clear that there was a need to give every member of staff a much more direct involvement in the work, with the ability to contribute their own ideas and to participate more in the development of the gardens. So this year all the staff were allocated their own garden or feature to tend, as their special responsibility. If Tony Blair had been in charge he would have called it 'stakeholder gardening'. Now they can decide what is planted in their own garden, what new features should be introduced and generally how they should develop. The gardens are 'rotated' each year, so that everybody builds up their skills and gets a new challenge each year.

~

The challenge for everyone in January was to get all the work done in horrendously wet conditions. With the water table high, after not just the January rains but also a whole preceding year of seemingly endless rain, every part of the gardens was sodden, with water lying in patches every time it rained again. This, of course, delayed all the important work of refreshing the borders, replacing plants and preparing the soil in the vegetable gardens. What could be done, however, was the hard-landscaping work.

The first hard-landscaping task, which was necessary not only to beautify the gardens but also to ensure that they conform to the rigorous statutory safety requirements demanded of a visitor attraction, concerned the paved paths in the Ornamental Kitchen Garden, which had begun to rock and to sink. This was inexplicable to Nick at first, because he had seen Geoff on television, with three million witnesses, laying the paths on concrete. Geoff was good at this and he demonstrated, in his usual helpful way, exactly how to do it to provide a path that would last for ever – and if Geoff had laid it you could bet your life it would. But when Nick lifted the sinking slabs he discovered that although the two Geoff had demonstrated on television were solid and secure, because they had been laid on concrete, the rest were laid on sand. This was presumably because Geoff ran out of time to do the job properly and the remainder of the programme would have been held up without a completed path. It is, of course, perfectly legitimate to lay paving on sand, but it can't be expected to last many years – as Nick discovered to his cost. So all the paths had to be lifted and laid again, this time permanently so that no ankles would be twisted as visitors walked around.

A problem in the Alpine Garden also had to be addressed. The Alpine Garden was one of the first features Geoff ever built at Barnsdale and because Barnsdale was in the very early stages of construction he had to use whatever land was immediately available. So he built the Alpine Garden on the lowest part of the land and as a result it floods every time there is a winter like the one we had this year – and alpines, like me, intensely dislike having wet feet. So Nick and Sue decided that this part of the garden would have to be drained. This entailed raising further stretches of paving, digging a long trench and laying a drainage pipe to discharge into the ditch at the edge of the property. The interesting thing, however, was that despite years of bad drainage the plants appeared to be thriving, which perhaps suggests that alpines are a lot hardier than the experts have led us to believe.

And the glory of the garden lives on. – Iris and Derek Hopkins, Cotgrave

Winter brings the sometimes arduous task which Jon refers to as 'clearing through'

As the rain continued its remorseless assault it became apparent that a similar problem existed in the conifer bed. Conifers, like alpines, will not tolerate waterlogged soil, so another drainage operation had to be got under way, to discharge the water into the same ditch. This is the kind of work that goes entirely unnoticed by the visitors because, naturally, they have no idea that it's been done; it also adds nothing to the well-being of the business. But it is essential if the gardens are to remain as attractive and magnetic as they have always been.

Dave Dawkins had problems with the rain. Dave, otherwise known as Dave the Druid, is the vegetable supremo – and he really is a Druid. In fact he's the one and only Druid we have at Barnsdale. Perhaps because he is a Druid, he has a love of Mother Earth that is genuine and true, and the joy of his work shines from his face like a beacon. He has no other requirements for complete contentment than the opportunity to live in harmony with the soil, to have sufficient money to live a simple, non-acquisitive life and to have his own wooden shed, to which he retreats from time to time when bad weather dictates. Having met Dave, with his quiet smile, kindly eyes, and endearingly cheeky sense of humour, I think that if I were to find religion it would have to be Druidism. The man is a walking advertisement for its goodness. A retiring, self-effacing man, Dave feels that Geoff is a hard act to follow and worries about meeting the same high standards that Geoff met; but he shouldn't worry, for his work is immaculate and he repeatedly produces vegetable gardens that Geoff would have been proud of.

Dave's problems began when he was double-digging his allotment. Dave is in charge of all the productive gardens at Barnsdale, having all the small television gardens to care for as well as his large expanse of Allotment. He found that as soon as he dug the first trench it filled with water, so rather than damage his beloved soil by consolidating it with his feet, he had to abandon the work. Dave is a good digger, paying meticulous attention to 'digging level', as Geoff always preached. A good 'level digger' should be able to leave a piece of ground so level that it only needs a tickle with a rake to get a perfect seedbed. In fact, Dave claims that he once received a call from the Crucible Theatre in Sheffield, who run the World Snooker Championships, saying that they were unable to hold the championships there that year so could they hold them on his digging, please? Perhaps just a small pinch of salt needed here. The water table had risen so high that covering the soil in the vegetable gardens with

ABOVE Dave is never more content than when double-digging his allotment, enriching the soil with a healthy dose of farmyard manure RIGHT Betty trims the edges of the lawn to keep them looking neat and tidy

polythene, effective in most years, was totally ineffective this year because the water was invading from below as well as from above. As a result, everything in the vegetable gardens was late except for a few seeds sown under cloches.

The weather also gave Sue problems with the pots that normally adorn the outside walls of the coffee shop. She had grown some unusual plants, to avoid the predictable pansies, and the finished pots looked wonderful when they were first planted up in January. Bursting with primulas, grasses, sedums, salvias, alpines and sage (no onion), they were redolent of a glorious and optimistic spring. But, after they had been beaten by driving rain and pounded by high winds, by early February they looked as though they belonged in a hostel for battered plants. Fearing the arrival of Social Security, Sue removed them to be replanted and replaced when the weather improved – which at the time looked as though it could be just as the season ended in October.

~

An irksome feature of inviting visitors into your garden is that they have feet – nearly all of them having two each! And they use them unmercifully to trample the grass. Well, of course they do. It's an open garden and nobody expects them to do anything else. But, naturally, as

they walk from garden to garden, they follow the tracks of the people who have preceded them. Measures are taken to protect the grass, with green, toughened-plastic portable paths, but these are not aesthetically suitable for all areas. Additionally, to prevent them from creating yellow patches, they have to be moved every two days – a tedious and back-aching job. Even then visitors stray off the paths to examine a plant or a feature, as they rightly should, so the grass is hammered hard during the season. The result is that worn patches appear in places as the season progresses.

Consequently a job that must be done at this time of the year is the repair of the lawns. Fortunately the odd spell of dry weather broke the interminable rainy periods, which meant that all the worn areas could be lifted and new turf laid before the first visitors arrived. Most visitors do not realise that around 30 per cent of the grass they are walking on is actually only a couple of months old.

There is one part of the garden where plastic paths wouldn't be appropriate: that is across the middle of the formal lawn that Geoff called 'Versailles' after an inspiring visit to the gardens of the palace of that name in France. The whole idea of this long, straight lawn is that it carries the eye down to an elegant stone urn at the end, and to have this vista interrupted by a long strip of plastic is just not acceptable. So the area where people cross the lawn was laid with hollow concrete blocks sunk to ground level, so that they couldn't be seen, and then sown with a hard-wearing grass seed.

The lawns were also spiked to improve aeration and drainage, with a powerful machine that drives spikes into the ground and retracts them as it moves forward. It's an impressive sight, as long as you keep your feet well clear. Sand was then brushed into the lawn and, as Geoff would have said, 'The job's a good'un.'

It is not all that unusual to receive a complaint or two, particularly towards the end of the season, saying that the grass doesn't look as good as it did when Geoff showed it on *Gardeners' World*. Well, that's partly because television always enhances colour and contrast but also because Geoff didn't have 120,000 feet walking on it every year. But you have to be careful how you say that, for fear of upsetting valued patrons.

~

Whatever the weather, this year was set to be a big one for Barnsdale because of the building work in the offing.

There were plans for an extension to the coffee shop, in order to make it big enough for an expanding volume of visitors and to provide a separate space to present talks and demonstrations for the great number of really enthusiastic gardeners who visit the gardens. The extension might make life slightly harder for Konnie Trewerne, one of the lynchpins of

Needs more orange and purple.
– L. Balcer, London

Most enjoyable – everyone pulling together in the midst of building – gardens look good, even in March. – J. Smith, Nottingham

Cleaning the coffee shop pays real dividends in enticing visitors in for some refreshment

life in the coffee shop, who keeps the place like a new pin, but she will take it in her stride, as always. A good-natured, bustling soul, she is more house-proud of the coffee shop and the other buildings than most people are of their homes – and that's not easy with hundreds of visitors each week trailing mud and bullets all over her floors and generally behaving as though they have just come in from the garden – which, of course, they have. She's one of the unsung heroes, is Konnie, an unseen sprucer and polisher whose work artfully entices people into the coffee shop and the shop. Judi Knight, the coffee-shop supervisor, will have her work cut out when things are happening in the new meeting room, but if her present performance is anything to go by she'll eat it before breakfast.

A new, brick-built shop was also planned, to replace the large wooden shed that Nick, his lifelong pal Tony, and Mick, a local jack-of-all-trades, built when the nursery first opened in 1990. This was to be surrounded by a new tarmac-surfaced car park, so that the existing pot-holes would no longer threaten the springs of cars. The plans for the shop had been drawn up by an architect because the last time Nick presented his own hand-drawn plans to the planning department they laughed him out of the building. One lives and learns. The furniture and fittings had all been chosen, as well as names for each of the rooms in the extended coffee shop so that people attending talks or demonstrations could be directed to the appropriate place.

The outcome of the planning application was now eagerly awaited by Nick and Sue. It had already been resisted by Exton Parish Council, who claimed that the buildings would be seen from the road – despite the fact that they were to be low and unobtrusive as well as shielded by a wide and dense planting of trees: to see them one would actually have to walk past, for a brief glimpse through the entrance gate, and not many people do that. Drivers going past would have to risk death by craning the neck as the gateway flashed by – it wasn't exactly Canary Wharf. The Parish Council's attitude was hard to understand, because at the height of the season Barnsdale employs up to fifty local people and provides business for all the surrounding hotels, bed-and-breakfast establishments, pubs, restaurants and shops. Nick was fairly confident that the county planners would recognise this and was losing little sleep over it, although it was still a nail-biting time.

The planning meeting was due to be held in March and a local builder, with whom they had had a previous good experience, was lined up, ready to go as soon as permission was granted. If consent were given a Portakabin would arrive on Wednesday morning and electricians were due to wire it up in the afternoon. The old shop would be cleared on Wednesday and demolished on Thursday. On Friday the building of the new shop was set to begin. The operation was planned like D-Day. So everyone had fingers crossed with a vengeance that planning permission would be given.

The talks, demonstrations and workshops that would be held in the new coffee shop (planners permitting) would be presented sometimes by 'names' in the gardening world, sometimes by skilled amateurs and sometimes by Nick or Sue or other members of the Barnsdale staff. So word went out to the staff that they should spend some careful cogitation time dreaming up subject matter, the idea being that the whole team would get involved in the enterprise. Of course, none of this could start until the following year, because the new shop was not yet built, but Nick and Sue were planning early so that they could get cracking as soon as possible.

Such staff involvement was part of a developing management culture that Nick and Sue are gradually putting into place. There has, in the past, been too high a turnover of staff for comfort, a problem only too common in small businesses where there is a distinct limit on the extent to which one can progress. There can only be one head gardener and if he or she stays it shuts off the opportunity for promotion for anybody else. The only solution to the problem is to try to enhance job satisfaction by making each member of staff the master of his or her own destiny, by getting them to think continuously about ways in which their job can be improved. This will then be rewarded, not by money, as this will be seen to be divisive, but by time off. Mind you, this won't work with Dave Dawkins: he'll be at work even if ordered, on pain of death, to stay away.

Nick and Sue had decided that mementoes of Barnsdale would be sold in the shop this year, so they were spending a good deal of time researching what was available and suitable. In the back of their minds all the time was the certain knowledge that Geoff was looking over their shoulders and would vent his celestial spleen if they allowed Barnsdale to be demeaned with inappropriate stock. They decided that in addition to postcards of views of the gardens there would be mugs, pens, pencils and similar items for sale, all bearing the Barnsdale motif. They then had to decide what to charge. This called for what they called 'research' but some may call snooping. They visited several other local visitor-attractions, including Peakirk Bird Sanctuary, Twycross Zoo and Oakham Museum, and, with some degree of subterfuge, they sneaked round their shops, making notes of the prices. They received some curious glances during this process because they neither entered the attraction nor bought anything from the shop; if there had been a Neighbourhood Watch person in any of the shops Nick and Sue would probably have been followed home. Eventually they pitched their prices somewhere in the middle.

Another exciting development was the forging of a new relationship with the Royal Horticultural Society (RHS). The Barnsdale gardens were now to be open free of charge to RHS members which, since the RHS has 285,000 members, Nick and Sue hoped would increase attendance. While these visitors would not contribute anything in terms of entry fees, it was hoped that they would increase turnover in the nursery, particularly as it specialises in unusual plants, which Nick and Sue expected to be of great interest to RHS members. The RHS, of course, advertise this fact to their members, which is another significant publicity boost.

An early 'score' here, in terms of advertising Barnsdale, was an RHS press release about a garden to be built at Chelsea by members of the Thames Valley Horticultural Society, who were avid fans of Geoff and were inspired by the gardens at Barnsdale and Geoff's passion for cottage-garden-style planting. As a touching tribute to Geoff, they were going to build a courtyard garden based on the design of the Courtyard Garden that Geoff built at Barnsdale and incorporating many other ideas – particularly from the Cottage Garden – that abound at Barnsdale.

Advertising in general was being stepped up this year, with a view to attracting more coach parties as opposed to cars. Of course people in cars are always very welcome, but it has to be a fact that fewer can fit inside a car than in a coach, and the car-parking capacity was now at its maximum. The number of coaches had begun to drop off a little the previous year so an increased level of advertising was essential. The fall in attendance may well have been due to the appalling summer, but no risks could be taken. The dilemma was that, while Nick and Sue wanted to encourage coaches, too many coaches would mean too many visitors and, as always, numbers have to be restricted to ensure that everybody has a peaceful and tranquil day out; the last thing visitors want is to be herded round with hoards of people. So the number of coaches was to be strictly limited. Gardening groups were to be targeted by mail and a database set up so that their attendance could be encouraged and monitored.

The Barnsdale web site was flourishing. Designed and built by Steve, Nick's elder brother, who continues to administer and maintain it month by month, it has proved to be extremely popular, with a larger than normal number of 'hits', perhaps because of the 'News' page, which gives details of new developments at Barnsdale, the 'Tips' page, which is constantly updated with tips and crafty ideas sent in by amateur contributors, and the 'In the Gardens' page, which is a weekly diary of the jobs that have been done in the gardens.

Preliminary work began on the souvenir guide to Barnsdale, which needed to be brought up to date and reprinted. All the photography and the design was to be done by Steve, who would also be busy each month taking pictures for the resplendent Barnsdale calendar, which was to be printed in readiness for the Christmas demand.

All the publicity and marketing work is done by Nick and Sue in the evenings and what's left of their weekends during the season. They aim to get as much as they can completed during the winter months, in order to free themselves during the spring and summer so that they can spend a little time gardening.

~

Work in the glasshouses and polythene tunnels was, of course, unaffected by the weather.

About fifty containers are planted each year in a polythene tunnel, starting with the hanging baskets and moving on to the bigger standing containers as the plants produced for them mature. The containers sit, or hang, in the warmth and comfort of the tunnel until all danger of frost is past. Just before the plants go out the tunnel is a sight to behold and the scent is enough to knock you over.

The alpine house, always of particular interest to visitors, was stocked with new plants and generally spruced up.

Cuttings and seeding of new perennial plants for the gardens and for the nursery took place as usual in the glasshouses and would continue as the time became right.

The nursery is run by David Mellows, a local lad, who has fingers as green as grass and he just loves his plants. He used to be a

LEFT The immaculately clipped topiary spirals in the Courtyard Garden make a stunning architectural feature ABOVE Cleaning up plants ready to go for sale can be a cold job for the nursery staff

garden-centre manager but decided to come to Barnsdale to be nursery supervisor, taking a drop in salary, just so that he could get closer to the growing process. So he's keen, skilled and invaluable – just the man the nursery needs. I'm told that all the plants stand to attention when he begins his inspection in the morning, but that may be an exaggeration.

Alas, work in the glasshouses was plagued by regiments of mice which scraped at the top of the pots and seed trays, presumably to get at the seed. They even had the effrontery to gather fallen clematis heads and build them into a nest on the heated blanket. So war was declared and traps were set to get rid of them. It's a sad thing to have to do, for they are pleasant little creatures, but needs must when the little devils drive.

There was a big effort this year to increase the stock of penstemons, particularly *Penstemon* 'Geoff Hamilton', as the previous year it had been difficult to keep up with demand for this lovely plant. *Viola* 'Barnsdale Gem', a 'sport' discovered in the gardens by Geoff shortly before he died, also had to be propagated in high volume, for the same reason. Cuttings were taken from stock plants overwintered under glass and cuttings would be taken from plants outside once there was enough growth and go on throughout the year.

There were plans afoot to change the way the development of new plant stock would be done in future. Just up the road from Barnsdale is Exton Nurseries, in a lovely old walled kitchen garden that must have supplied the 'big house' at one time. It has a quaint old potting shed, a wonderful north-facing cold store where apples and other fruit are stored in the winter and a little 'bothy' where Dave and his wife Margaret live in much-coveted isolation.

A real touch of old Victorian England. Nick and Sue had recently taken on a lease of the nurseries and six acres of land, so as to make more room for sales at Barnsdale and to have a bigger area of glass without spoiling the peaceful aspect of the gardens.

Because of the nurseries' sadly neglected state, there is a lot of investment and work to be done before they can become fully operational. Eventually it is intended that they will become the site where all the nursery stock and new plants for the gardens are grown. By early 2001, however,

ABOVE The jumble of pots and equipment in the potting shed belies the orderly nature of the nursery
OPPOSITE Betty must be constantly on the alert for the emergence of weeds

already half of the land had been planted up with stock which had been 'lined-out' for growing on to supply the nursery. A couple of the old glasshouses had been rescued and refurbished; sadly, the others are, like me, beyond redemption. A polythene tunnel had been erected and was in continuous use for growing young and more tender plants and as a 'standing-out' ground for plants raised at Barnsdale and needing to grow on until they reached saleable size. Serried ranks of plants in pots stood to attention on the gravel base, awaiting their call to action.

Varieties which are not yet for sale in the nursery will be grown on at Exton Nurseries rather than being planted in the gardens. The snag with planting new varieties in the gardens is that visitors see them and want to buy them, but they can't do so until sufficient stock has been propagated so the new varieties have to be kept on the secret list until it has.

All the plants at Exton Nurseries are cared for by Margaret Dawkins, Dave's wife, who is an uncannily similar replica of Dave in terms of her dedication and hard work. She's ably assisted by Joan Lakeland and between them they care for their plants like children.

The landlord for Exton Nurseries is Viscount Campden, who manages the estate on behalf of the Gainsborough Trust, and he has turned out to be an extraordinarily good person to work with. He and his estate workers have done all kinds of work that they didn't really need to do – laying gravel, cutting grass, even clearing up the rubbish that arose from the clean-up of the land. Who said the aristocracy never get their hands dirty?

Since the Barnsdale nursery specialises in unusual plants, it is obviously necessary to seek sources of unusual seed. This is obtained from the Henry Doubleday Research Association's Heritage Seed Library, a fruitful source of many old and rare vegetable varieties; Plant World in Devon; Secret Seeds; the RHS; the Alpine Garden Society; the Hardy Plant Society and other garden societies, all of whom have many unusual varieties.

Nick is keen that some seed from Barnsdale grown from the vegetable seed obtained from the HDRA Heritage Seed Library should be returned to augment their stocks and complete the circle of 'give and take'. But if Dave grows vegetables until they run to seed he has visitors wondering why he has been so lax about harvesting his produce. So Nick has had a large notice made, which in effect says, 'It's OK. It's *meant* to be like this.'

Suttons, Dobies and Unwins all supply annual seeds free of charge early in the year, so when these are displayed, mainly in containers and baskets, a notice accompanies them explaining where the seed came from. Catalogues are also available so that visitors who have seen a plant and liked it can easily find where to get the seed. I think that's what the marketing men call a 'symbiotic relationship'.

~

Thankfully, in late January the weather eased and there was even a glimpse of a strange pale orange disc in the sky that some of the older members of staff recognised as the sun. This provided the all-important break that was needed if the gardens were to be opened on time. So all but compassionate leave was cancelled and the troops stood to, heavily armed with scaffold planks, forks and spades, ready for battle. On the word of command they set to with a will, spreading a thin layer of well-rotted manure on the borders and forking it in lightly, working from the boards all the time to avoid consolidation of the wet soil. They pruned the roses and cut back the large-flowered clematis, cut the dead growth off the herbaceous plants and cut back shrubs that had grown too much into one another. They cut back hard specimens like the eucalyptus, the yellow-

After flowering the shrubs are pruned back to keep them under control and to ensure a good display next year

ABOVE New planting in the Drought Garden usually takes place in early spring or late autumn RIGHT General maintenance is a constant, though vital, task if the gardens are to be kept looking their best

leaved elders and the purple-leaved varieties of elder to promote new growth, but left plants that are grown for the colour of their stems, like the cornus and the rubus, until April, so as to get maximum effect from their colour. The willows were left altogether, as they were being grown on over a period of two years to provide withies for a living willow arch, which was to be planted at the end of March or early April behind the Country Garden. This was inspired by the Paradise Garden that was built at the HDRA in Geoff's memory, so it has a particularly poignant meaning as well as being a very interesting feature.

Cutting back, however, was kept to a minimum in the gardens because close planting and good ground cover is the gardens' style. This was Geoff's favourite planting style. He didn't like expanses of bare soil that could be growing something beautiful, so the garden has the look of a family of plants all snuggling up together for comfort. There has been the occasional complaint about this, too. Some people believe that a closely planted garden is not as attractive as one where everything is widely separated and that the intermingling of plants is a sign of neglect. But this was definitely not Geoff's philosophy, so Nick, ever mindful of the need to maintain the integrity of Geoff's legacy, which is what most people come to see, is resolute about maintaining the gardens in the way in which Geoff would have done. It is very difficult to please all the people all the time.

While some worked on the flower beds, in the Allotment Dave, with his usual manic enthusiasm, finished his double-digging; and he also planted potatoes for a really early crop. He did this in a hot-box, which is a bed filled with horse manure topped with a layer of soil. The horse manure is supplied by Sue, not literally, of course, but from the two horses she keeps behind the barn. She gleefully wheels steaming barrows up the path to the Allotment, almost invisible herself in clouds of horsey fumes, a big cheesy grin on her face. There's self-sufficiency for you. Victorian cloches are then used to shelter sowings of radishes, carrots and the like. The hot-bed seems to be intensely interesting to visitors because it demonstrates one of the many ways in which the season can be extended to provide a seamless flow of vegetables all the year round.

Last year when Dave grew potatoes in the hot-bed he ended up with enough for a couple of good meals for the family, but then there was a hiatus while those he had planted under polythene sheeting on his deep beds caught up. Deep beds are a boon to any gardener, but especially those with only a little space. They are simply beds that are double-dug, incorporating lots of farmyard manure and pea gravel if the soil is heavy, a maximum of four feet wide, so that they can be reached from either side, and as long as you like. They do not have to be double-dug each year, of course. Mine have now become so fertile that I just spread a layer of rich compost on the top and draw a cultivator through the soil. What they provide is a hugely nutritious area where plants can be planted a lot closer than in conventional beds and yield is at least doubled. To avoid his potato hiatus this year Dave planted some tubers into buckets, which will reside in one of the polythene tunnels, to provide – he hoped – a continuous crop until the end of May, when those on the deep beds would be ready.

This impertinent Druid, taking on Geoff's mantle, challenged me to the traditional potato race to see who can come up with the first tubers. I warned him that his methods would have to be a lot better than Geoff's if he was to beat me and that he would not have the opportunity to tell the great British public that he won when he didn't, as my infamous brother used to. Perhaps, I thought, my wounded pride and outraged sense of injustice will be healed at last.

Dave was also busy raising lettuce, tomatoes, aubergines and peppers in the greenhouse to supply the coffee shop when it opened. Like the old Victorian gardeners supplying the big house, it is a matter of pride for him that he maintains a constant daily supply of fresh produce to feed the hungry visitors, which, because it's organic, tastes good and helps to keep them living longer, so that they keep coming back. He is also charged with the

Enjoyed ourselves very much. Appreciated chatting to Dave. The food was excellent value. Thanks. – Martyn and Diane Davis, Leicester

responsibility of raising all the other vegetables, so he had his work cut out in his greenhouse as well as on the land, when the weather would let him.

~

After this brief interlude of sunshine, the whole of February was an endless round of shower-dodging or just having to work inside. But there was no shortage of indoor jobs to be done.

A vital job that can be done indoors is the making of new plant labels, much of which is done in winter but which continues throughout the year. The aim is to label all the plants, so that if people would like to have one they can make a note of the name and buy it in the nursery. Now 99.9 per cent of visitors, like you and me (well you, anyway), are honest, good-hearted people who come to Barnsdale solely for a good day out. But occasionally the odd scoundrel turns up who, with malice aforethought, quietly wanders around pinching the labels from plants that he or she has in their own garden. These are big labels and each one has a sizeable stake on it, so it must be a work of considerable ingenuity to conceal several of these about the person. But the British have never been short on ingenuity and conceal them they do. Nick has even been approached by a visitor, on the verge of tears at the desecration of Geoff's legacy, reporting a venerable old lady, with an innocent face like that of your own grandma, digging plants up from the garden and stuffing them into a plastic carrier bag. Unfortunately he was unable to find her – had he been able to he would have taken serious action, venerable old grandma or not. But this year he asked the staff to resolve to be more vigilant and try to persuade recalcitrant visitors to buy their plants and their labels in the nursery.

The cleaning and replacement of signs is another important task that has to be carried out before opening day. They are washed and if damaged or worn they are replaced. Nick and Sue listen carefully to the comments of visitors and feedback from the staff, picking up ideas for new signs that are needed either to clarify an aspect of one of the gardens or growing methods or to supply further information. It is noticeable that, while there are a lot of helpful signs, there are none that say 'Keep off the grass' or 'Please take your litter with

LEFT Pruning is an ever-present task, but in winter shrubs must be cut back to reduce their size and to encourage new growth ABOVE All the signs are cleaned as a routine part of the spring sprucing up session

ABOVE Shredding the huge piles of prunings and trimmings which accumulate during the year is a hugely satisfying, if noisy, task RIGHT The plastic paths, which protect the grass from a multitude of feet, have to be rolled up and moved regularly to prevent the grass from yellowing

you' or 'No hawkers or circulars'. The only warning signs are those that are there to protect people. This is because, as Geoff used to say, gardeners are always nice people. There is absolutely no need to try to regiment them or preach about good behaviour. Well, they're nearly always nice people – just some who steal labels.

The signs are made by Ralph and Yvonne Bell, who live in Peterborough and were one of Geoff's valuable discoveries. During the filming of the 'Cottage Gardens' series for *Gardeners' World* he interviewed Yvonne, who has a beautiful modern cottage garden. During a break he was griping about the fact that he couldn't get a decent sign-maker. 'Oh, we can do that,' said Yvonne. 'It's what we do for a living. We're Peterborough Signs' – and they have been doing it for Barnsdale ever since. Geoff was always a master of serendipity.

An enjoyable job for wet spells is that of shredding all the organic matter that can't be composted. All the prunings, trimmed tree branches, cabbage stalks and the like are stored in a big lean-to building at the back of the gardens to keep them dry. Shredding is done all season, but the bulk takes place in winter. The material is fed into a big industrial shredder, which chews it up and spits it out, at a great rate of knots, in the form of a finely ground material that is ideal for mulching. This is normally composted for a few months, mainly so that the colour tones down to a pleasant brown, and then it's spread around the gardens wherever needed.

This is the time of the year, too, when all the machines used around the gardens are sent down to a local engineer for maintenance: mowers, strimmers, hedge-trimmer, chain-saw, rotovator – anything that has moving parts. This is essential if the gardens are to be properly maintained. Having machines break down at crucial times can cause disaster, so it's a big job – and a big bill!

~

ABOVE Snowdrops are lifted from the Woodland Garden while still in flower, for replanting around the bust of Geoff in the Memorial Garden RIGHT All the paths are raked each morning to provide a pleasant walk for visitors

At the end of February the weather miraculously relented for a spell. There was some sense of foreboding that it would be a short-lived spell and that winter had not yet departed altogether, so there was now an air of urgency about the work still to be done.

It is at this time of the year, with a month to go before the first visitors rush through the gates, that attention has to be given to the paths. Normally the paths are plastered in mud, which has to be scraped off and covered with a substantial layer of granite chippings to provide a smooth, dry walking surface. This year, however, before any work started, the plastic mats that are used to protect the grass from visitors' feet had all been gathered up and laid over all the paths, completely covering them. At the end of February, when most of the dirty work of the winter had been done and all the muck had been carted away, they were simply rolled up and carried away for cleaning, leaving the paths in the condition they were in at the end of the season. A light sprinkling of chippings was all that was needed to make them perfect again. This simple idea not only saves a great deal of time but saves a great deal of money as well. The best ideas are always the simplest. When the gardens are open these paths are raked every day, to ensure that they are pristine for visitors to walk on.

After the plastic mats had been cleaned they were relaid on the grass to protect it, especially on the new turf. They have to be laid in pairs, with a gap between, both to enable people to walk side by side and, more importantly, to make a sufficient width for a wheelchair. Mobility for the disabled and the elderly is greatly helped by the fact that the entire garden is almost completely flat, so nobody has to struggle up and down steep slopes as they do in some gardens.

Many disabled people come to the gardens and Nick and Sue planned to build a special garden for the less mobile this year, to show that all but the most severely disabled can enjoy the tremendous pleasure and contentment that a beautiful garden can bring. The design had already been discussed with the landscape designer Adam Frost. He had gone away to put the ideas down on paper, in the form of a rough plan, and these would be discussed and agreed so that work can start as soon as the conditions are right.

The pond, the Bog Garden and the stream were cleaned and all the dead leaves and weed removed – a miserable job

Judi prepares her weekly order for the coffee shop

on a cold winter morning. Many of the plants in all three features had to be thinned. The easiest way to tackle this job was to grasp the nettle, don the waders, take the whole lot out and replant them. The final job, believe it or not, was to pressure-wash all the pebbles so that they returned to their bright, white selves.

A difficulty that Barnsdale has that not all gardeners have is deer. The gardens are invaded constantly by muntjac, which gnaw the bark of trees, eat whole branches of shrubs and generally create havoc. Muntjac are small, solidly built Asian deer with antlers and tusks. How they got here we have no idea. Illegal immigrants, perhaps. Because they are very shy they do not appear to be dangerous and only arrive at night, but they are a considerable nuisance. The seven acres of the gardens have had to be fenced against them to a height of about six feet. They seem to know that a good food source lies beyond the fence and they are constantly seeking ways to get in, so each year this fencing has to be checked and repaired. It was hoped that the fencing would be enough to keep them out this year; if not, further measures would have to be taken. The difficulty is that too much fencing would give the gardens the oppressive look of a concentration camp, so there is a limit to what can be done.

~

Thanks to the hard work of all the staff, Nick and Sue's confidence was justified and all the pre-season tasks were done in time – and on 1 March the gardens opened.

Judi, who runs the coffee shop, was ready with a wider than ever range of food and refreshments, and eager to meet the demands of a surging crowd.

Sadly, Terry the noble car park attendant had to retire this year on health grounds. He was a tremendous asset to the gardens because his ebullient character lifted the spirits of the visitors as soon as they arrived. 'Welcome,' he would say. 'Welcome to Barnsdale' – and with a flourish he would direct drivers to their spot. People would stand at the coffee-shop window and watch in wonder as this flamboyant man charmed visitors with his flowery speeches of welcome. He was much loved and will be greatly missed.

There was still, though, the welcoming face of Sylvia Ridley, the wife of one of the Oakham vicars. She has a wonderfully warm smile and just a slight tendency to mother people, so that they feel important and cared for – a tremendous asset and all too rare these days. She doesn't so much *run* the shop as *reign* over it, a bit like the Queen but with better-behaved children. She shares her days with Jackie Mellows, who is the wife of David the nursery supervisor. (Nick and Sue, Dave and Margaret and Jackie and David make three husband-and-wife teams at Barnsdale.) Jackie is a typical product of Lancashire, strong, determined and capable, with a dry sense of fun.

But the hoped-for flood of exuberant visitors strolling around in the glorious spring sunshine turned out to be a dribble of cold, wet visitors braving the elements but doing a good deal of sheltering in the coffee shop. Although the weekends were fairly busy, the attendance during the week was more than disappointing.

In addition to having bad weather this year the country was being ravaged by foot-and-mouth disease, which – as well as leading to the awful sight of burning funeral pyres of slaughtered animals around the country – necessitated the closure of all footpaths and the cancellation of many events and attractions located in the countryside. Although Nick advertised the fact that the gardens were still open, both in newspapers and journals and on the Barnsdale web site, there was no doubt that the epidemic was deterring people from visiting the countryside and reducing dramatically the numbers visiting Barnsdale.

We could only hope that the disease would shortly be brought under control and that things would get back to normal. All businesses of this kind are at the mercy of the weather, and Nick and Sue were philosophical. There was still a lot of season to go, so spirits were still high.

~

One of the great delights for me, when wandering in the gardens, is that I am occasionally recognised by visitors, either because of my picture in one of the earlier books I have written about Geoff or simply because we looked so alike, and people tell me of their admiration and love for Geoff. I have to say, it does the old heart good.

Two visitors I met in early March who braved the cold and the wet were Maria Clairemont, who was fairly new to gardening, and her mother, Heather Delargy, an old hand. They had come all the way from Lincoln. They visited Barnsdale at this time of the year (making prudent use of a token from *BBC Gardeners' World Magazine*) because Maria, who had just bought a new house, thought it would be a good time to see the structure of the gardens rather than being seduced by a sumptuous display of flowers. Clever thinkers, these gardeners! They found the

OPPOSITE The emergence of the first of the graceful, pendulous catkins is a welcome sign of approaching spring

layout of the gardens useful as a means of idea-gathering, because it is divided up into the small gardens that Geoff used for his television work. Her mother was a keen fan of Geoff's, claiming that she never missed a programme. She was able to connect the gardens with her memories of the programmes and this really raised her enthusiasm. For her, the visit seemed more of a pilgrimage than a visit. She even went to the shop to buy one of my earlier books and ran back, pen in hand, for a signature. My totally undeserved, second-hand celebrity strikes again!

In mid-March I met David and Valerie Hope, two intrepid visitors who had ventured out in the rain, the wind and the biting cold from the shelter of their base camp in north London without any form of survival equipment. They were about to move to a new house in the country and were looking for ideas for their garden. Having lived in leafy suburbia for some years, they had not been inspired to garden very vigorously, but now that they were to have a new country garden the obsession was beginning to bite. They had always been avid Geoff-watchers, spending each Friday night with him. I detected a note of disappointment in Valerie's voice when I pointed out that there were several women that Geoff would spend Friday night with, but she took it on the chin. They still watched *Gardeners' World* and felt

> *We liked Geoff! – but live next to Alan.*
>
> – Pam, Richard, Sue and Tony,
>
> Beech, Hampshire

that, while the style of presentation had inevitably changed, old Titchers, following a very hard act, was doing a good job, though they had some reservations about the plethora of makeover programmes. Mind you, I rarely speak to anybody who doesn't say that, yet they attract enormous audiences. So where are all the people who watch them? It's like trying to find somebody who voted for Margaret Thatcher. Nobody admits to it yet she seemed to have occupied government for an awful long time. In my view, Alan Titchmarsh will always hold top spot as long as he continues, like Geoff, to advise people about what they have to *do*, week by week, in their own gardens.

Valerie made the point that Geoff made to his producers many, many times – that she didn't want to see large expanses of beautifully and expensively maintained gardens. Geoff knew that that wasn't what most people could relate to. She wanted to see – as Geoff wanted his viewers to see – how small gardens could be turned into little tracts of tranquillity, which was why she had come to Barnsdale. David was surprised at how different the small gardens he had seen on television looked in reality. Not that they were any less impressive, but the sense of scale is enlarged on television and he was fascinated to see how much variety and interest could be packed into such a small space. Having been together to the Chelsea Flower Show, which they felt was very contrived, they found it immensely refreshing to find Barnsdale so unpretentious and full of ideas that were all achievable by the ordinary gardener. They both felt it was a great day out and well worth the trip from London. So another pair of satisfied customers, leaving with a bundle of germinating ideas.

~

Behind the scenes, now that preparations for opening day were complete, attention turned to the preparations for the two major shows at which Barnsdale was to be represented: the Gardeners' World Live exhibition at the National Exhibition Centre in Birmingham in June and the Hampton Court Palace Flower Show in July.

The show tunnels had been filled with plants. Sue is fortunate to have access to the plants in the sales area and the stock grounds at Exton Nurseries, where she occasionally finds a plant that has, as she puts it, 'made something of itself' and is suitable for addition to the show tunnel. The plants were being cosseted and nursed so that they would reach their peak in time for the shows. The tunnels are lit with sodium lighting that shines day and night to fool the plant into thinking the season is later than it is to encourage growth. The lighting must be controlled to ensure that the plants are at their best just at the right time. All the plants, which included various types of grasses, hebes, hemerocallis, hostas, ligularias, crocosmia and salvias and a wide range of others, were 'tidied up' and would be fed on a high-nitrogen feed to bring them on fast.

The Cottage Garden Society were planning a courtyard garden for the Chelsea Flower Show this year and they asked Sue to put some *Viola* 'Barnsdale Gem' into the show tunnel for bringing on in time for Chelsea. This being an example of the kind of serendipity which happens to observant gardeners from time to time and so an ideal subject for a cottage-garden exhibit.

Each year Sue has sole responsibility for the show-plant operation and she nurtures these plants as dedicated show plants, under glass or polythene all the time, so that she can be sure she has the biggest and best plants possible. They have to be perfect in every respect – there can be no distorted flowers, no brown patches on leaves and nothing wilting or even looking a bit tired. These are the Marilyn Monroes of the plant population at Barnsdale and when you look at the wonderful display they make in their prime you almost feel they know it.

Because Barnsdale is a young garden it isn't geared up to exhibit at any more than these two shows, but this year Nick and Sue were going to tour some of the other shows so that they could weigh them up and decide whether or not to expand this side of the business. It's good publicity for the gardens and they can sell a lot of plants. In particular they were thinking that they might exhibit at Tatton Park, where they might do a 'back-to-back' garden, but the rest was, as yet, in the melting pot.

They were not going to enter the Chelsea Flower Show. Nick and Sue have always had reservations about showing at Chelsea, because it has a much more grandiose ethos than exists at Barnsdale. It seems to have grown to be a show about design whereas Barnsdale is a garden about plants and ordinary people, setting out to demonstrate some ideas and garden plans that they can carry back with them to their own gardens. I had a feeling that this view might change as Nick and Sue got more experienced and confident, simply because Chelsea

LEFT This mature *Prunus* 'Imose' was the first tree to be moved into the new Japanese Garden RIGHT Once lifted the *Prunus* 'Imose' was planted at the foot of the bridge, to conform to the Japanese custom of providing shade for those who pass over the bridge and also to cast shadows on the still water

is the premier horticultural show in the world and it would become impossible to resist making a Barnsdale entry. Anyway, Barnsdale would have a representation at Chelsea this year with the Barnsdale-inspired entry of the Thames Valley Horticultural Society.

~

Work on a new Japanese Garden started this year. Its most prominent feature was to be a pond, spanned in the middle by a traditional Japanese bridge. There are normally two opposing styles for Japanese gardens – a minimalist style, with dry plants and small trees set in gravel, and a much more lush, floriferous style, with a profusion of flowering and foliage plants. Because the Barnsdale gardens are partly designed as a learning experience from which people can pick up and carry back ideas for their own gardens, the Japanese garden was designed so that it is artfully split into two, to demonstrate the two differing styles, with the bridge as a dividing feature.

By mid-February the pond had been dug out but the liner was not in place, the bridge had been built and a *Ginkgo biloba*, the maidenhair tree, and a *Prunus incisa*, the Fuji cherry, had been planted. A mature *Prunus* 'Imose' was moved from the main garden to the Japanese Garden in mid-March and planted at the foot of the bridge so that the delicious scent could accompany you as you cross – a sensitive Japanese tradition. This initial stage was finished by the end of March, but completing a garden of this kind is a long, painstaking job and would probably take two years.

~

One morning in early March, Dave found himself greeted by a pale imitation of the sun; so, as soon as the soil was dry enough for him to work on it, he erected his pea netting in the Allotment and planted out some peas that had been started under glass. He had plundered the treasure chest of the HDRA Heritage Seed Library for a variety called 'Prince Albert', which was curiously introduced in 1842 to commemorate its namesake. Seemingly no giant sequoias or rare and ravishing orchids for poor old Albert – just a humble pea. But it is a giant pea that grows to six feet and has a prolific crop of sweet, white-seeded peas. Dave also

One of the best gardens we've seen and a great memorial to the man himself. Lots to learn here.

– Jan and Martin Langcroft, Ongar, Essex

sowed directly, in soil that had been covered to keep it dry, 'Sugar Crystal' and another pearl from the HDRA, 'Purple Podded', which produces plants five to eight feet high with striking purple flowers and deep-purple pods. Dave was growing these mainly as a spectacle for the visitors, who are always fascinated by unusual discoveries. For this reason he grows a lot of other unusual vegetables – 'Purple Falstaff' Brussels sprouts, 'John's Purple' carrots, 'Bull's Blood' beetroot and many more.

He put me to shame by planting some broad beans that had been raised under glass – though I reckoned I'd catch him up, even with a late sowing. Here, again, he had found some gems from the HDRA. 'Crimson Flowered' is a wonderful sight when in full flower and has small, upright pods which are cooked and eaten whole. 'Martock' was the mainstay of the medieval diet, named after Martock in Somerset, which is now a small town but in medieval times must have been little more than a collection of humble dwellings, a church and a manor house. The beans have a rich, meaty taste and were used on fast days, giving rise to the expression 'Martock men be full of beans! If you shake a Martock man he rattles.'

Dave is a gambling man. He realises that planting and sowing this early is risky, but he always feels the urge to 'have a go' and he backed up his experiment with a reserve batch that still sheltered in his greenhouse. He also planted 'Martock' beans and 'Purple Podded' peas in the Ornamental Kitchen Garden, to show some striking colour among the summer flowers.

When planting, Dave employed two of Geoff's innovations which are by now well known and widely used, and are as effective as ever. The first was to erect in the Parterre Garden one of Geoff's famous tunnel cloches, stretching polythene over alkathene water pipe and burying it in the soil at either end. Under this he was able to sow carrots, lettuces and radishes. The second was to grow peas in a length of plastic guttering, in the greenhouse. Later he would dig a shallow trench outdoors, lay the guttering in it and slide out the guttering from under the peas, leaving them all in place without disturbing the roots.

Apart from the beans, Dave was wisely holding back most of the vegetable plants he had started in the greenhouse because it was simply too cold and wet to plant them out. Like any sensitive gardener, Dave looks upon his plants as friends – and he believes that nobody would allow their good friends to stand outside in the cold when there is a warm chair for them by the fireplace. Dave keeps records of the weather year by year and he told me that rainfall last January was 6.5 ml and this year it was 26 ml. So no wonder that things were late.

~

Then, amid all the endless rain and the turmoil of worrying about the planning application, the foot-and-mouth epidemic and the desperate shortage of visitors, Dave delivered a bombshell: he was going to leave. He had been head-hunted by a gent with a large country house and a tempting walled vegetable garden, which he wanted Dave to care for. Nick and Sue talked it over with Dave, trying to emphasise the advantages of staying at Barnsdale, and finally Dave, never a man to make a hasty decision, went away to think about it. He thought while he dug and he thought while he sowed and he thought while he potted, but, he told me, it wasn't until he sat in his greenhouse, cup of tea in his hand, and looked out at his freshly dug soil that he thought, 'No, I can't leave this. This soil needs me.' I believe he felt it deep in his soul. Barnsdale had become his life, his love and his companion and he just couldn't turn his back on it. So he ambled across to see Nick (Dave always ambles; even when he's running he ambles) and delivered the good news, to much back-slapping and cries of relief. The Barnsdale vegetable gardens were back in safe hands.

~

Eventually, after much nail-biting, the great day of the planning meeting arrived – Tuesday 13 March. Nick and Sue duly took themselves off to the council chamber in Oakham. I tried to talk them into taking a banner with them but, I'm sorry to say, they chickened out. Well, they're only young! They settled themselves down for the meeting, with sweaty palms and hearts hammering. The chairman of the planning committee, Rob Lacey, lives in Exton. He was also, rather ominously, a member of the Exton Parish Council who had initially raised objections to the plans. But in the event it was all rather an anticlimax. Rather than carrying the objection forward, the chairman just stated that he drove past the site every day and could see no reason to turn down the application. It was put to the vote and nodded through. Nick's heart, which had once had a dicky valve and objected strongly to all the hammering it had been asked to do, quickly calmed down and he and Sue left with broad grins on their faces. Nick immediately contacted his builder, electrician and the Portakabin supplier and they were in business.

Frustratingly, the Portakabin didn't arrive until the afternoon of 14 March, so the electrician had to be put off for half a day, but by the end of the following day the shop was reopened, albeit smaller, but only temporarily. The old wooden shop was dismantled carefully, to be re-erected elsewhere to provide more dry working space. As soon as that was done the building work started in earnest. Personally I was sad to see the old shed go. It seemed like losing an old friend; but business is business, as they say, and the show had to go on.

With the start of the building programme heavy expenditure also began. Nick had timed the building work to coincide with the resumption of the cash-flow generated by the influx of visitors. But March had been a disaster. The foot-and-mouth epidemic had had a catastrophic effect. Ninety per cent of telephone callers enquiring about the gardens asked if the disease has closed the gardens down. There must have been a great number of people who didn't telephone but just stayed away. This, combined with the cold, wet weather, reduced visitor numbers during March by 56 per cent on last year. March is never a good month for visitors, but even the small amount of income that normal visitor numbers generate would have kept the wolf from the door.

There was nothing for it but for Nick to make a trip to the bank manager, armed with his figures, and explain. Much to his relief, he found his man to be understanding and supportive. It's wonderful what a couple of billion pounds' profit will do to ease the pain of banking. Now what was needed was an easing of the foot-and-mouth restrictions and a warm, dry Easter.

Nick spends his final few days in the rather dingy, but homely, old wooden shop before it was replaced by its bright and airy successor

CHAPTER TWO

~

A Slow Start
to a Glorious
Spring

~

April and May

A Slow Start to a Glorious Spring

~ *April and May*

There is a wonderful feeling at Barnsdale that, whatever the elements can throw at it, it is always going to regenerate from its dormant, slumbering and rather drab winter hibernation and suddenly burst forth into a delightful series of sensations and surprises. So it was this year.

Hopes for a warm and dry Easter appeared to be an impossible dream, for it was a dismal start to spring. A steady, unrelenting downpour continued unabated for the first two weeks of April, dampening not only the land but also the visitor numbers. A desultory and courageous few trickled through the gates, wrapped defensively in sweaters and waterproofs and armed like warriors with umbrellas of all shape, sizes and hues. The brave Barnsdale workers were amazingly unfazed by the conditions, working determinedly through the rain as though ignoring it would make it go away. To add to the rain there was a biting Arctic wind, which seemed to carve its way through to the bones of staff and visitors alike. If this continued for much longer the business would suffer terribly.

But suddenly, on Good Friday, as if anticipating the celebration of the Resurrection, the dark clouds limped back to Hades and the sun burst through. It was clear that Michael Fish and his merry band had conjured up one of their seemingly never-present 'ridges of high

ABOVE The lovely blossom of the Umbrella Plant OPPOSITE The formal expanse of grass, bounded on each side by huge borders was inspired by a visit to Versailles and was the first garden Geoff ever built at Barnsdale

pressure' and the nation rejoiced. Spirits soared and there was a general feeling that the gardens were back in business.

The sun appeared to revive the spirits of the plants as well and there was a rapid acceleration in the speed of flowering and growth, with the spring bulbs emerging and all the early-flowering plants giving a hint of what was to come. They say that nature always compensates for its sins and it certainly seemed that Apollo, the sun god, and Ceres, the goddess of crops, had been disciplined and were now atoning.

The long shrub and herbaceous border which Geoff called Versailles can look uninspiring during the winter. There are some striking evergreen shrubs and when the hoar frost is on the leafless branches of the other trees and shrubs it is a breathtaking sight; but when all the herbaceous plants have died back and there is a lot of bare soil to be seen and the weather is wet and dull, it is easy to believe that it will never look good again. But now the trees and shrubs groaned with burgeoning buds and the plants that had gone into hibernation began to show their finery. Birds were beginning to sing and the quiet shuffling sounds among the undergrowth betrayed the presence of small animals, emerging to take the air. The great numbers of buds on the trees and shrubs heralded a good year for blossom, as long as Jack Frost kept his icy hands off during the remainder of spring.

All this growth alerted the staff to the need to provide their hungry plants with some grub. So they fed all the borders with pelleted chicken manure, a well-balanced, organic, slow-release fertiliser which Geoff introduced to Barnsdale some years ago. In doing so he helped its innovative manufacturers, Rooster, to build a large and thriving concern from very small beginnings. Unfortunately they now face some uncommonly inequitable competition, in this so-called global economy of ours, from the state-subsidised Dutch poultry industry, which transports huge amounts of manure from battery houses to this country, where the competition turns it into cheap pellets which are promoted as organic but do not bear the insignia of the Soil Association. It's a tough life for the genuinely organic manufacturer. Nick describes the chicken manure as 'odorous' – and, even though I am an avid user myself, I have to agree – but the smell is quickly dispersed and the pellets will go on doing their job for many months. Personally I like the smell, because it reminds me of my old farming days, but it certainly is an acquired taste.

At last we've visited the gardens of the man who inspired us. Lovely! Lots to take home.

– Jacky and John Willoughby, Holton St Mary, Essex

Another good organic feed used in the gardens is made from comfrey, an attractive but highly invasive plant, which is grown at Barnsdale in an 'isolation ward', away from the normal borders, where it could easily become difficult to control. Many organic growers prepare a special bed surrounded by grass so that the overspill can be mown out, but at Barnsdale there is sufficient confidence in Dave's eagle eye for this to be unnecessary. When the leaves are harvested, which they are frequently during the year, for the plant is as tough as old boots, part of the crop is used in the compost bins, where it is mixed with the grass cuttings to aerate them

During the building of the new shop all sales took place in the temporary Portakabin, which was usually heaving with eager visitors

and prevent them from forming a solid, slimy mass. The other part is immersed in water, where it is left for a week or two, after which it has become a fine, balanced liquid feed.

The unaccustomed sunshine resurrected the visitors, who poured through the gates just as they had done last year. It was hard on them when they arrived, because they all had to troop into the tiny Portakabin that was the temporary shop to buy their entry tickets. Those who bought plants at the nursery had to endure the crush for a second time when they paid for them. But not a single complaint was received. I've often said this but it warrants repetition: gardeners are almost universally good-hearted and resolutely cheerful people. They seemed to be determined to enjoy their visit to Barnsdale, whether they liked it or not – although there is no doubt that the vast majority leave feeling inspired with a new enthusiasm.

~

A group of visitors who were effusive in their praise for the gardens were Ian and Leslie Laughton and Carol and Alex Taylor, who live close to each other in a little village called Scalford, near Melton Mowbray. They were all devotees of Geoff's programmes and this was not the first time they had been to Barnsdale; like many other visitors, they returned frequently to absorb new ideas that they could carry back to their own gardens. They agreed, with rueful smiles, that the work on their gardens was never going to be completed: it was always evolving and changing as they had new ideas and plants outgrew their homes. But this they saw as the fascination about being a gardener – the ever-changing nature of the work and thus the view.

I'm sorry to say that they were pretty scathing about the current crop of television gardening programmes because of what they saw as their superficiality and their instantaneous nature. Alan Titchmarsh, an old and much respected friend, will crucify me for printing this but I plead that I am simply reporting the news. They all agreed that gardening was a long-term process, requiring a great deal of skill and a lot of plants, as opposed to an overload of decking, paving and trendy designs. I was glad to hear that Alan was planning a new, down-to-earth gardening programme.

Of particular interest to them were all the 'cheap and cheerful' artefacts that Geoff had introduced to Barnsdale and which are religiously maintained by Nick and Sue – the polythene cloche supported by alkathene water pipe, the 'carry-cot' cold frame made from an orange box, the elegant wooden 'beehive' compost bins, the wooden obelisk – an idea he brought back from a stately home – and many others. Geoff did all those things because most of his audience were unable to afford hard-landscaping materials, or even mature plants bought at garden centres, but it has to be said that in these more affluent days more and more people *can* afford instant gardening. Whether or not they *should* miss out on all the joys of self-sufficiency and the evolution of their garden is a different matter. I wasn't prepared to enter into that argument with the kindly Laughtons and Taylors.

They were very much traditional cottage gardeners, the Laughtons and the Taylors, which was why they loved Barnsdale so much. They didn't like the idea that new gardeners were daunted by thinking that they had to invest in things like £1000 stone troughs and they told me so in broad Leicestershire accents and no uncertain terms.

'Take an old stone sink,' said Ian, 'slap a bit of cow muck on it and before long you won't know the difference. I've done it and it looks really good.'

'Mind you,' interjected Alex, in a dry, serious voice, 'you should have taken the taps off really!'

Leslie talked about her mother, who, just after the Second World War, had three quarters of an acre and looked after it on her own, working all hours that God sent. Desperately needing to supplement her husband's wages, she grew vegetables and managed to provide a constant supply – and, what's more, provided the finest diet in the land – enough for her to avoid buying them, and everything in season, too, because there were no deep freezes in those days. She also grew flowers in abundance, nearly all self-seeded and haphazardly placed but leaving an impression on her daughter's mind that was fondly cherished to this day. Such productivity combined with cottage-garden-style planting was, of course, Geoff's dream of paradise and it is well demonstrated in the sublime gardens at Barnsdale. Small wonder that these gentle, contented country people loved to wander in the gardens, to be transported back to a more peaceful life.

~

At the end of March Gavin, the head gardener, left for pastures new, heading for a job in a garden centre in the wilds of sunny Ilkley. Nick and Sue had a long discussion with Jon about his taking on the post of head gardener. Jon felt a distinct lack of confidence about his ability to master the job. He is an intelligent, enthusiastic young man but he was very conscious of the weight of responsibility this position would place on his broad but untried shoulders. Nick, however, had no qualms about Jon's skills and to allay his fears suggested that he could gradually build up his confidence through one-to-one training and experience. Thus he was appointed. Of course, even when Jon felt sufficiently confident to manage the enterprise himself, Nick and Sue would still be in general command, but they would withdraw from the day-to-day technical management and let him make his mistakes, fall into a few traps, find his own way out of them and, in doing so, build a solid base of experience and skill.

In the event, young Jon took to the job like a duck to water. The staff all like and respect him and, despite the fact that there was still a trace of the cradle marks on his bottom, he found himself able to master the technical complexities of the job rather better than he had thought. He also loves to talk to the visitors and they seemed to respect his advice and knowledge, which, after all, is what it's all about. Oh ye of little faith!

Wonderful! NO DECKING! What gardens are all about.
– P. King, Redditch, Worcs

The dense, arching stems of *Exochorda wilsonii* bear a mass of white flowers amid clusters of dark green leaves

Darmera peltata, the Umbrella Plant displays its pale pink and white flowers in spring, before the foliage appears

By the end of March enthusiasm for Nick and Sue's staff development philosophy, in which the staff were being encouraged to participate in the development of the gardens, was palpable. In fact Nick said that it was almost embarrassing, with a constant bombardment of new ideas coming from the staff in a seemingly endless stream. If only some of the autocratic industrial managers I have met would learn this simple lesson. Life would be happier for all concerned, and they would have the small additional perk of creating a lot more job security for themselves. Not a bad deal in my book.

~

Lawn-mowing began in the second week of April, with the first cut aimed at just shaving a little off the top, so that the grass would receive less of a shock and not suffer from that 'short back and sides', jaundiced look which so many people seem to favour. Ben Claridge, who had recently started work at Barnsdale on a three-month trial, suddenly showed a dormant lawn-mowing skill that nobody had suspected. Not only did this engaging young man race through the work, but he also displayed a skill with stripes that would do credit to Lord's cricket ground. At the end of his stint on each of the many lawns and grass paths he would stand for a moment's 'admiring time', blissful smile on his face, deep in the satisfaction of a job well done. From this small beginning I had a feeling that young Ben is going to derive a lot more satisfaction from jobs well done. If only we could get the gardening bug to infect all young men, I'm sure we would solve a lot of our social problems.

His aptitude also solved a worrying problem for Nick. With the looming cash-flow problems he was anxious to keep staffing to a minimum, but nobody has yet bred a variety of grass that understands the problems of cash-flow and it obstinately continues to grow. Of course the grass, though unnoticed by most visitors, provides the setting for every border, so it's imperative that it's kept in good order. Nick was on the point of having to ask Dave to abandon his vegetables for one day every week – which he would not have liked – when Ben, like Henry V, valiantly stepped into the breach. If ever there's another Agincourt my money's on Ben.

The time had now arrived to remove the layers of horticultural fleece which had been protecting plants like the standard bay trees and the gunneras, and the warm sunshine meant that the large pots in the Gentleman's Cottage Garden could be planted up.

There was an almost audible groan of relief from all the plants in the garden, as though they had served their time and were now released. It was amazing how quickly they seemed to be transformed from their earlier dull and lifeless condition, put on their glossy coats and showed what they were made of. They seemed to be running to catch up for lost time and, once more, the garden put on its smiling face.

~

In 1999 the inspector from the Health and Safety Executive had arrived, unannounced, at the gardens and asked Nick if she could see the Health and Safety policy statement. Nick's eyebrows disappeared into his hairline and he stammered, 'Our what?' He and Sue knew nothing of their obligations for the health and safety of the visitors and had made no preparations whatever. Fortunately this particular inspector was a wise and effective woman and she guided Nick through the requirements, with an ominous warning that she would be back. Now Nick claims to be paranoid about safety. Everywhere he goes he looks for protruding branches that could damage eyes, uneven paving that could twist ankles, unmarked steps that could trip unwary visitors – anything that could represent a hazard – because he is conscious of the fact that it would take only one serious accident, arising from his neglect, to close the gardens down. Unfortunately this means that he and Sue often have to resort to measures that wouldn't be taken in the average back garden. For example, they have painted yellow lines along the lovely old paving that forms some of the steps – not aesthetically pleasing, but then neither would a garden littered with dead visitors be aesthetically pleasing. It's just the lesser of two evils.

Now the H&E inspector returned, because, on the previous routine inspection, she had discovered that the frozen foods for the coffee shop had been stored in the same building as the tubs of chicken manure. All food and all chicken manure are tightly sealed in plastic containers but, reasonably in Nick's view, this was not seen as good practice, so they had to be separated. This involved the provision of another building, but Nick was philosophical about it, his paranoia having now taken a firm hold. I envisioned the need for some help and began to search for a suitable therapist. But when the inspector returned the new arrangements passed with flying colours.

When one considers the number of people who pass through Barnsdale every year it is surprising how few complaints there are. The worst was voiced not to Nick or Sue but to the *Daily Mail* in 1999. A lady wrote to make the complaint, as a few others have before her, that many of the shrubs were growing into one another and she thought this untidy and neglectful, implying a lack of respect for Geoff's ideals. She also claimed that some of the grass in Geoff's Memorial Garden was unmowed and the cercidiphyllum tree that had been planted next to the grave of his faithful old dog, Moss, was on the verge of death. The letter was quite vitriolic and, unfortunately, demonstrated some lack of horticultural knowledge. Apart from the fact that close planting was the very style that Geoff had aimed for when he first built the gardens, the unmown grass was actually a wildflower meadow under construction and the cercidiphyllum tree was just getting established – it was a gawky child, just about to blossom into a beautiful teenager. But the press, ever eager to trumpet abroad a perceived failure, printed the letter with a banner headline proclaiming Barnsdale's paucity of style and lack of respect for Geoff's ideals – a hurtful calumny which Nick felt deserved a reply. First, however, he spoke to Geoff's old and trusted producer, John Kenyon, who advised him not to write an outraged reply but to be humorous with his explanation. This Nick did, but the *Daily Mail*, with typical attention to fairness and even-handedness, printed a small extract, right at the bottom of the letters page. We shall continue to take the *Guardian*.

Both Nick and Sue try hard to impress on visitors that if they see something they think could be improved, or if they have an idea to contribute, or if they just want to ask why something has been done as it has, they should ask. They will always get attention and if Nick and Sue see something that needs changing it will be changed. They recognise the fact that no gardener, however well trained and experienced, knows it all. Although in most cases there will be an explanation as to why things are as they are, they are very much aware that there are some exceptionally knowledgeable gardeners who visit Barnsdale and they are always eager to pick up any new ideas. Because visitors are invariably gardeners and therefore, as night follows day, nice people, they are often reluctant to ask questions, especially if they appear to be critical, but that's 50 per cent of the reason why the staff are there and visitors should never shrink from enquiry. And, frankly, it's a bit daft to go writing to the press *before* raising it with the staff – they could even get a sensible explanation.

~

Once the sun had begun to show its friendly face around the gardens again it became a particularly busy time for Dave in the vegetable gardens. Early April is, of course, a major seed-sowing time. Apart from the usual brassicas, lettuce, beetroot, spinach and the like, Dave likes to go in for some more unusual adventures. Hyssop, for example, is one of his favourites: a perennial evergreen shrub with leaves that sport oil-bearing glands and flowers that have useful medicinal properties. They can be made into what Boots the Chemist would call an 'expectorant' – a soothing relief for colds and sore throats. I don't know why Dave was growing it, because he never has a cold or a sore throat, but he is a man of great caution. The leaves are also a mild sedative, another thing that Dave, the most relaxed man you could wish to find, doesn't need. Perhaps when he loses the Great Potato Race he will!

He was also growing sorrel, purslane and rocket, all spicy additions to liven up a dull salad, and kohl rabi, a strange, truncated little brassica which can be made into soups to die for. A great innovation are the new 'mini' vegetables – cabbage, cauliflower, turnip, carrots and beetroot – all of which Dave sowed in early April and then in succession. These are particularly useful for gardeners with limited space and are specially bred for deep-bed culture, as they can be grown at much closer spacings than normal vegetables. They have the added advantage that, because they are picked when still small, they are much sweeter than their big, rough cousins. A plant Dave was growing which I confess I had never heard of was *Stevia rebaueiana,* a herb whose leaves are used as a sweetener for hot drinks – it makes a substitute for sugar and is a lot better for your health. Dave swears by its delicious taste, although he warns of an unpleasant saccharine aftertaste if the leaves are eaten raw. The seed is hard to find but a little diligent searching or a look in the *RHS Plant Finder* will provide you with a little treasure. Dobies Seeds certainly used to include it in their catalogue – it may be worth an enquiry.

Dave raises a good number of surplus plants because Barnsdale suffers agonisingly from wildlife. Given that it is a strictly organic outfit that tries its hardest to encourage wildlife, that may sound a peculiar thing to say; but there are some unwelcome intruders which are very difficult to control. Mice not only, as I have mentioned, create havoc in all the glasshouses but even outside in the gardens they feed voraciously on the bulbs, which often have to be replaced, though now they are usually raised in pots and planted later. For some unaccountable reason mice don't seem to attack growing plants, so this seems to have solved the problem.

Visitors amble contentedly past the allotment, clearly enjoying a relaxing day out

If the mice don't do a good enough job they call in reinforcements and the rabbits invade, particularly in the vegetable gardens. There have been occasions when Dave has painstakingly planted rows of brassicas only to discover the following morning that they are nothing but a row of leafless stalks. The Allotment is fenced against rabbits, with wire netting, buried to the depth of one foot six inches and then angled out at ninety degrees for a further eighteen inches, to prevent them from burrowing, but this still doesn't stop them. They have, like any intelligent rabbit, discovered the gates, which can't be protected adequately so, without a 'by your leave', they just gatecrash the party. Because of a rapidly increasing population, with great regret Nick decided that they had to be controlled so he called in Mick the Pest Control. I had the same problem in my own garden recently and solved it by covering the crop with horticultural fleece, which seemed to deter them, but this option is not open to Nick as it would hide the very things that people have come to see.

Even though the deer have now largely been excluded with strong fencing, the occasional desperado still manages to break in and eat anything in sight, including the bark from the trees, which often have to be replaced. Parts of the box hedges in the Parterre and the Knot Garden had to be replaced this year because they gave themselves up as supper for the deer.

Moles seem to gather in regiments to burrow under the grass, throwing up their own ramparts on the way. They are trapped in humane traps and released in an appropriate area, far from Barnsdale. Careful thought is given to the location for their release, which provides interesting possibilities for mischief, so if you intend to visit you had better be on your best behaviour or you may one day discover a mysterious mole invasion.

Dave likes to plant his potatoes with religious fervour, always on Good Friday if weather conditions allow – and this year they did. There were no incantations as he planted them but, like most good gardeners, Dave silently worships his 'taters'. He planted them on a bed of well-rotted muck, so that they could get a flying start, although planting was difficult because of the wet soil conditions. But they went in well and Dave was pleased, retiring to the sanctuary of his shed with a self-satisfied smile on his face. The potatoes were joined that evening by parsnips and six varieties of carrot. Later still that evening Dave planted the excess potato tubers in the new vegetable garden he had prepared close to his little bothy up at Exton Nurseries. If he ended up with enough he would distribute this substantial crop among the staff and friends, just as Geoff used to do.

In the Allotment there were eight varieties of early potato, nine varieties of maincrop, six varieties of Brussels sprouts, four varieties of kale, two varieties of kohl rabi, three varieties of cabbage and two varieties of turnip. More would undoubtedly be added at a later date. I got the feeling that the large number of different varieties grown in all the productive gardens – the Allotment, the Parterre, the Elizabethan Garden and the Ornamental Kitchen Garden – were not only for the visitors and for experimental purposes but also (mostly) because Dave, like a mad professor, has an enquiring mind and is always trying something new.

He protected most of the brassicas with two-litre plastic bottle cloches, not so much against the weather as to guard against the multitude of rabbits, which would have their wicked way with them if no security was in place. The plastic bottles didn't look too pretty, but it was a simple choice between rows of bottles or no rows of brassicas. Pigeons were now making their presence felt and had already destroyed a row of sweet peas, so he netted the remainder and sowed a new batch in the greenhouse. They would be late, but should still provide a good show.

But Dave, I am sorry to report, has nightmares about his carrots. Some of us have nightmares about our children or paying the mortgage or redundancy, but Dave has nightmares about carrots. He seems to have great difficulty growing a decent crop. If it's not poor germination, it's slugs, and if it's not slugs, it's rabbits – and so his carrot-driven neurosis grows. Nick has tried to assure him that Geoff couldn't grow carrots either, but it seems to

Dave's bottle cloches keep birds and rabbits from his precious brassicas

be little consolation. What distressing crosses some of us have to bear.

This year he tried a layer of wood ash between the rows to deter the voracious slugs – a ploy based on the premise that ash is an irritating surface for them to crawl over and is said to block their slime glands, so well worth a try. Dave, though, suspected that they'd probably regard the wood ash as an hors-d'oeuvre and eat that as well. However, I can report that early carrots were harvested in the third week of April, to the sound of fanfares and the beating of drums.

As an example of how the season can be extended by the judicious use of cloches and

Brings back memories of Gardeners' World as it was. – Sandy Whitlock, New Milton, Hants

fleece, not only were early potatoes harvested from the hot-box from the second week in April onwards but also the coffee shop received a regular supply of lettuce, radish and spring onions, from the hot-box as well, ensuring that the salads for the visitors were as far removed as possible from those served in fast-food outlets. Melons were now planted in the hot-box, which must be the most productive square yard in the whole garden.

In one corner of the Allotment, next to Dave's shed, is a small pen containing three chickens. I think these are a concession to Sue, a farmer's daughter, who clearly feels the need to keep in touch with her roots. They can hardly compete economically with the great burden of vegetables that comes from the Allotment – after all, they only manage one egg a day between them – but they provide a source of amusement and a little more bucolic pleasure for the visitors. I do wish, however, that we still had Herbert, Geoff's hen, which would have been the star of the show. It had an injury to its leg and it would goose-step around the yard like an SS officer. We thought seriously about making a uniform for it, but the difficulties were too great and the RSPCA were hovering. It would also force an entry through the cat-flap in Geoff's back door and eat the cat food, but no disciplinary action was taken. It died in comfort in a warden-controlled pen, but its spirit lives on.

~

Wandering down the path next to the Allotment on Easter Monday I met Mr and Mrs Laidler from Lincoln, who had discovered the gardens by pure fluke, having set out to see Rutland Water. They had known about Barnsdale for a long time, from watching *Gardeners' World*, but hadn't realised that it was in this part of the world, thinking that it was in Yorkshire. I cruelly pointed out that they must be thinking of Barnsley, but I think I was doing them an injustice. Anyway, they saw the signpost and, wondering if this could be the television Barnsdale, they set off to find out.

They live on a cliff top, Wellington Edge, which overlooks the Lincoln valley and has some spectacular views but is plagued by high winds and heavy weather, which limits what they can do in their garden. So they were interested to know if they could get some ideas from Barnsdale. Unfortunately for them, though, Barnsdale lies in a very sheltered position – bounded on one side by the majestic trees which line Exton Avenue, leading to the gates of the Earl of Gainsborough's estate, and on the other by a high hawthorn hedge – so they had not succeeded in that part of their mission.

However, they found plenty to enjoy at Barnsdale. Like many of the visitors, they loved the fact that the gardens were set out in small plots as they were shown on television. They were able to relate them directly to their own garden and gather ideas to beautify their own plot. They were particularly attracted to the fact that the layout gave rise to the intrigue of, as Mrs Laidler put it, 'going round the corner'. They found great delight in the surprise of discovering something they hadn't expected – a feature that Geoff was particularly keen to build into his garden, though I often felt that, rather than going round the corner, he was more likely to be going round the bend.

They raised with me the fact that they would have liked to see a little more description and history about each garden and I have to say that I agreed with that and said I would raise it with Nick and Sue. For example, they were unaware of the fact that Geoff started with just the television gardens but bought the large adjacent plot when he and Nick started the nursery. At that time visitors to the nursery would ask if they could visit Geoff's television gardens, but he valued his solitude very highly and would never allow it. So, never wishing to alienate his devoted audience, Geoff built replicas of all the television gardens on the piece of land next to the nursery. Nick and Sue have now replaced and renewed most of these, to provide more variety, so the total area of garden has practically doubled in size.

Visitors are a constant source of delight and interest and I particularly enjoy meeting them and hearing their gardening stories. In May I met Margaret Hale, who had sent me an e-mail that said:

> *Hi Tony,*
> *Thoroughly enjoyed* Geoff Hamilton: The Complete Gardener. *Hope you'll write another one. You certainly brought fond memories of Geoff into our home. He's permanently with us in our garden as I can hear him giving me instructions on how to look after the plants. We visit Barnsdale every year and have the sweet pea, penstemon and rose dedicated to Geoff. I also bought Carol's [my wife's] botanical paintings of the sweet pea and penstemon, and would love one of the rose. If Carol has one could you let me know the cost and postage and I will send you a cheque. Thanks for writing the book on Geoff. He was and always will be the best gardener ever. He inspired me to take up gardening fourteen years ago at the age of fifty with his comment 'You can do this' and now I'm hooked!*
> *Regards, Margaret*

I often get letters and e-mails about Geoff but this one touched a particular chord, so I wrote back suggesting that we meet at Barnsdale when she and her husband Charles visited – and we arranged to meet in the coffee shop.

What I met were two bubbly Liverpudlians, with their enthusiasm for their garden shining like a beacon. Although now living in north Wales, both retired, they were each blessed with that typical 'Scouse' wit. Margaret told me that she had first noticed Geoff when she had been into a garden centre and heard the owner complaining about him. The previous Friday he had recommended the use of a sheaf of organic barley straw for cleaning the algae from ponds. The garden centre had been inundated with requests – and they didn't have any. This mirrored my own experience. I have lost count of the number of times I have been into a local garden centre or ironmonger's shop to be greeted with the words 'Your bloody brother!'

Margaret told me that they travel from north Wales at least once every year to visit Barnsdale, to remind themselves of the pleasure they derived from Geoff's 'hands-on' approach and to pick up more ideas for their own garden. 'I've got the obelisk,' said Margaret proudly, 'and the herb table, complete with a piece of slate to rest my cup of tea, and Charles has made me a planter that we've filled with the "Geoff Hamilton" rose from David Austin Roses.' Charles, it seemed, like many a husband before him, was the labourer, doing all the heavy work and the hard landscaping, while Margaret was the designer. A self-confessed ham at carpentry, he had simply followed the instructions in one of Geoff's books and the result was masterful. He also shyly admitted that he always asked for Geoff's posthumous approval before installing his work.

Beautiful and many useful designs. Lots of ideas. Thank you, Geoff.
– Sylvia and Jim McCawley, Denmead, Hants

One of the interesting points that Margaret made was that a visit to the garden is essential to get the things that Geoff did into perspective. She hadn't realised how small the individual gardens at Barnsdale were and how close they were in size and shape to their own. They showed me photographs of their tiny garden and it was an inspiration. Don't ever let anybody tell you that you can't do anything with a tiny space. If in doubt, contact Margaret and Charles. I know without question that Geoff would have been as pleased as Punch that I had this conversation and saw what they had done through his advice. It was exactly the inspiration he was trying to give to people. Margaret also confessed that she would sometimes take her cup of coffee out to her bench and herb table and talk to Geoff, asking for his advice about what she should do next in the garden. Our conversation warmed the old and vulnerable heart of a rather sentimental brother.

~

By early May spring had announced its return in no uncertain manner. Buds were opening and the ornamental gardens were beginning to show spirit-lifting splashes of colour and the promise of a blissful summer to come. The first swift was seen on 2 May, a sure sign of better things ahead.

All the fruit trees were in full blossom and straining their sap to supply a good crop of fruits of all kinds. There wasn't a single tree that didn't look as though it would crop its heart out, provided there were no late frosts. If it all set and there was not too great a summer drop, there would be enough fruit to feed the British Army. There are fruit trees in most of the gardens but my favourite is the small orchard close to the Allotment. As well as some highly productive trees it has some soft fruit, which stands in the shelter of the trees in small beds cut out of the grass. This now had a lush carpet of grass beneath the trees and looked especially romantic.

In the Ornamental Kitchen Garden, Dave was sowing and planting many new and interesting vegetables, which were mixing delightfully with their flowering cousins to form not only a harmonious mixture of colours and shapes but also the prospect of a productive crop to sensually tickle the palate. Dave always chooses the plants carefully to blend well with the flowers here – a practice whose success is demonstrated by the fact that many visitors don't even realise that vegetables are grown in the plot. Spinach, carrots, parsnips, globe artichokes, sweetcorn and many others gave fine architectural form to the borders, while ruby chard, climbing beans, crimson-flowered broad beans and red cabbage

The lovely *Prunus* 'Okumiyako' shows off its delicate white spring mantle. Its dark green leaves will turn a deep carmine red in autumn

provided colour. Marrows and pumpkins were planted strategically so that they would climb the trellis. While the fruit has to be supported when it becomes too heavy, this is a good way of making best use of available space. There is always a limit to your area of flat land, but if you grow upwards the sky's the limit.

There were also lots of fruit crops in the garden, all carefully chosen to fit a small space and to blend with the design of the garden and its planting. For example, one of the beds is bounded by step-over apple trees, pruned so that the main stems are horizontal and the tree is only about two feet high. The horizontal pruning encourages copious fruiting and this year the crop looked especially bountiful. The fences were clothed in climbing plants and fan-trained or cordon fruit, with the result that the fence itself could hardly be seen. The little hexagonal greenhouse housed some tomatoes, cucumbers and melons. A family who established a garden like this would have little need to trouble the greengrocer and they would get the pleasure of a colourful garden as well. That's what I call having your cake and eating it.

In the greenhouses attached to the Allotment the aubergines were attacked by greenfly, whitefly and red-spider mite, so the floors were being regularly damped down to deter the red-spider mite, which doesn't like humidity, and the greenfly and whitefly were being sprayed with insecticidal soap. It would take only an invasion by a hostile nation to complete the picture, but Dave was not yet filling sandbags as he felt the possibility was remote.

Dave was conducting a 'members' experiment' under the auspices of the HDRA, designed to test the effect of garlic in deterring aphids. 'Members' experiments' are small-scale experiments, rather than scientific trials, which arise from the interest of members who wish to examine more closely a bee they have buzzing around in their bonnet. The experiments are small because most members do not have the facilities to conduct a full trial, but they often reveal some very interesting results and sometimes go on to become full-scale scientific trials run by the HDRA. This particular experiment was being conducted with pot-grown aubergines. Two plants had been set aside, one being grown normally, as a control, and the other having a clove of garlic pressed into the compost to see if it would deter greenfly. Every week the greenfly infesting each plant were counted and recorded. I have to say that at this early stage in the experiment the one with the garlic looked much healthier than the one without it, but we would see.

Another HDRA experiment concerned the perennial runner bean 'Painted Lady'. Although this is a tender plant, it was expected to crop satisfactorily for several years – unlike the normal runner bean, which is an annual and will crop for one year only. So it had been

ABOVE LEFT A good crop of marrows will be ripened and stored for a winter delicacy BELOW LEFT Dave chooses one of Geoff's famous love seats to have his lunch and indulge in the satisfaction of some 'admiring time'.

planted out and later the crop would be weighed and compared with that of a normal runner bean. Then it would be lifted, to lie dormant under the protection of the greenhouse until it was time to plant it out again. Then the whole procedure would be repeated, to find out if it gives a heavier crop as it builds up size and vigour.

By the end of May there was a row of sweet peas in the Allotment, already in full flower. A deep carmine variety called 'Karen Reeve' was really spectacular and set off to perfection by its companion, the soft lilac 'Geoff Hamilton', a plant bred by Diane and Terry Sewell and dedicated to Geoff's memory. All along the bottom of the row Dave had planted a row of *Limnanthes douglasii,* the poached-egg flower, which not only gives a brilliant display of bright yellow and orange flowers but also attracts hover fly, which will hoover up aphids by the thousand. There had been a further two rows but these had been destroyed by guess what – rabbits. No wonder they are not regarded as cuddly little creatures at Barnsdale.

Lovely big onions!

– Mr and Mrs Frost, Ipswich, Suffolk

Grate! We had a lovely time. I liked the rose garden best.

– Mummy, Daddy, Samana, Rose, May, Sheringham, Norfolk

Work began on the design and construction of a new Mediterranean Garden. This was being built because the original was in the gardens immediately surrounding the house and, as this is still the home of Geoff's wife, Lynda, visitors have no access to this. It was to be a gravelled area, positioned to benefit from the maximum amount of sunshine and planted with sun-loving, semi-tropical plants. A *Cordyline indivisa*, which is known prosaically, and quite undeservedly, as the cabbage palm, was taken from the Paradise Garden, where it was getting too big for its boots, and divided. Part was replaced in its original spot and part was planted in the Mediterranean Garden. It is an evergreen plant with a single, unbranched stem which can grow to a height of twenty feet or so, has long, lanceolate leaves with red or yellow mid-ribs and in time will bear large, pendulous panicles of white flowers in summer and clusters of round, purple berries in autumn. It should be quite a sight, making a dramatic centrepiece for the garden.

Another garden under construction was the formal Knot Garden. The box plants that edge the beds were still immature and, because they were not ready for clipping, were looking very straggly. Nick and Sue hoped that the visitors would read the notice and understand that the garden is far from complete; without the sign there was the danger of just the kind of misunderstanding that could lead to a complaint. The Knot Garden is of a most unusual and captivating design, with four small gardens centred around a pond, which looks magnificent though is at present unplanted. The pond is formal in design, with four rectangular 'arms', each of which contains an elegant statue that gushes water from the top into the inky black pond below. The rippling sound of the water is soothing and peaceful. It is not hard to imagine a number of husbands contemplating with horror the possibility of some heavy expenditure when they get home.

The alpine house was just beginning to come into its own. Inside there is staging on either side on which alpines are displayed, some in pots but mainly growing from small hypertufa 'rocks'. There was a resplendent exhibition of colour from some delightful saxifrages, alpine penstemons, salix, serpilifolia, *Pulsatilla vulgaris*, rock roses and a host of others. Visitors should set some time aside for this because it can take an hour or so to fully take in the beauty of this art gallery of plants.

The Drought Garden at Rutland Water is heavily mulched in autumn to ensure that moisture loss is kept to a minimum

The Parterre Garden was looking full and productive. In the small beds, each devoted to one variety of plant, there were sweetcorn, onions, garlic, courgettes, globe artichokes, savoy cabbage, cauliflower, cardoons, broccoli, Brussels sprouts, herbs of all types and even some potatoes, grown under black polythene, which were well advanced – but not as far as mine. Dave was going to lose our bet and I suspected that panic was setting in. Nevertheless, he had certainly crammed a lot of good vegetables in a plot about half the size of the normal estate garden. So how can anybody who has access to a piece of land that size complain that food is expensive? And this little garden wasn't just a cornucopia of fine produce but it was also very beautiful into the bargain. All credit to Dave, even though his potato-growing skills could do with honing a little. My goodness, Geoff, you don't know what you started here!

At one end of this delightful garden there is one of Geoff's inevitable arbours, housing two chairs. Now the most glorious honeysuckle climbing over the top was providing not only the sights and smells of summer for passing visitors but also a good dense cover for small birds, who were supplying musical accompaniment.

In the Rose Garden the dozens of roses were preparing themselves to burst stunningly into life. Rich, healthy buds abounded, promising a sensational display, though as yet they were biding their time. There was nevertheless still a lot of colour in the Rose Garden, produced by a range of graceful aquilegias, set off by hostas and *Sagina boydii*, which forms a mound of tiny, bottle-green leaves. The deutzia, though not yet in flower, looked as though it had pledged a profusion of dainty white flowers this year.

The pergola that connects Versailles with the rest of the garden was burdened with laburnum just about to emerge as great drifts of golden yellow.

~

In the first week in May, maintenance work was carried out on the Drought Garden. This is a garden (its name seemed ironic after all the downpours and the mud) that Geoff established on the shore of Rutland Water in 1993. It was commissioned by Anglia Water to demonstrate how, with the right choice of plants, a garden can flourish without the

Every spring the borders are tidied and 'pricked over', to incorporate a good layer of farmyard manure

need for regular watering – though since it was originally built there has hardly been a great call for additional water. Though it is owned by Anglia Water, it is in a sense an outpost of Barnsdale: it is maintained by Barnsdale staff and regular visits have to be made to the site.

The planting programme was divided into three phases, so that Anglia Water could spread payment over a period of time – possibly for cash-flow reasons, although that takes some swallowing with this billion-pound company and it seems more likely that they didn't want the regulator to know that they had spent a few bob on plants.

The first stage of planting was now completed and labelling needed to be done. All the plant names were carefully noted so that engraved labels could be made for each one. Regular visits would need to be made to replace those that, as surely as night follows day, would gradually disappear.

At Barnsdale Marie Mitchell, who works part-time from home, spends an entire day every week making labels, but still all the plants are not labelled. This is not only because the labels are regularly pinched, but also because Nick refuses to label anything unless he is certain of the correct botanical name. Geoff, of course, planted thousands of plants and in the hurly-burly of his television work the labelling of many of them was overlooked and nobody now knows their names. Also it's by no means unknown for someone to buy a plant from a nursery or garden centre only to discover that it isn't the variety described on the label and this has happened at Barnsdale. Nick has thought of asking the expert Roy Lancaster to come across to the gardens for an identity parade of the Barnsdale criminals. His immense body of knowledge about plants would enable him to identify most, if not all, but the problem is that he would probably have to come every week, when the plants are flowering, which would be impractical.

But there was now another plan to help visitors to identify the plants they see in the garden and wish to buy from the nursery. Jon, head gardener and a dab hand at plant recognition, was starting to compile a catalogue of every plant in every border, as far as he could. From this work a computerised database will be built up so that, provided visitors can remember the garden the plant came from and its approximate position, they will be able to ask for it in the shop even if they can't remember the name. The staff will be able to identify it for them and if they recognise it from a picture the job'll be done. It will still be necessary to make the odd visit to the garden concerned to verify facts, but it should speed up the process significantly. And if labels go missing, as they frequently do, it will be possible to replace them immediately. It's a big job that will take a long time, but it will be invaluable when it's completed.

~

The building of the new shop had been going well. By the middle of May the roof was on and only the doors, the floor and the fittings remained to be completed. Nick was amused by the fact that just as everything was as good as complete the notification that the planning application has been successful came through. Rutland County Council's timing was, as ever, immaculate.

The extension to the coffee shop was just about finished. The opening talk was to be presented by Pippa Greenwood on 6 June and the builders were working a good deal of overtime to finish it in time. The tension was heightened by the fact that Mel, the builder, who is a specialist in this kind of work, has a daughter who was about to get married, so he kept having to knock off early to be measured for his suit, get his hair cut, get his nails varnished and so on, which only added to Nick and Sue's sense of frustration. But the work seemed to be under control and Nick was confident that all would be well, though Sue was a touch more cautious in her optimism.

Nick and Sue were delighted that Pippa had agreed to come, because she was a long-time colleague of Geoff's who took part in many *Gardeners' World* programmes with him. The

ABOVE There was a measured hurry to complete the new coffee shop extension in time for the first of the regular programme of talks and demonstrations RIGHT Shooting the new video, 'A Year at Barnsdale', took place each month, to build up a picture of what is done in the gardens throughout the year

talks were going to be a stimulating new adventure and Nick and Sue were looking forward to the first with a mixture of excitement and trepidation. They had planned it with the utmost care, so things should run smoothly – but you never know what the other Old Nick has up his sleeve.

The builders provided a good deal of amusement, not only for the staff at Barnsdale but also for the visitors. Like builders everywhere, they sang – and they sang very, very badly, a fact which seemed not to deter or embarrass them in any way but which gave rise to a number of broad smiles from passers-by. On one of the rare sunny days one of the young lads, aged about twenty-two, was throwing tiles up to his mate on the roof, his bare chest glistening in the sunshine, when three old ladies passed by, their average age at least seventy-five. One of them stopped to feel his bicep and said, 'Ooh, you're a nice boy, aren't you!' That really embarrassed him, neatly turning the tables on the builders' normal sexist approach, and the day was well and truly won. Well done, madam, you deserve an OBE.

However, the builders had a negative effect on a lady who visited with her husband, who was recovering from cancer and suffering from the debilitating effects of chemotherapy. He had been obliged to leave his job and face a very early retirement, so the poor chap was predisposed to be upset and emotional. They had come for the peace and tranquillity offered by the gardens – a little treat to reduce the pressure. They settled in the coffee shop, only to find themselves assaulted by the din of hammering and the noise of an angle grinder. Somewhat distressed, they had to move out of the coffee shop and try to find a quieter spot in the gardens.

Fortunately the lady mentioned to Nick that her husband was becoming upset by the noise. Nick – who is always conscious of the fact that the visitors are the top priority – stopped the building work immediately and directed the builders to another job, well away from the gardens. The result was that the couple had a quiet and absorbing time in the garden and, before they left, the lady sought out Nick to express her gratitude. She assured Nick that they would be back – and we all hope they are.

~

At about this time the BBC at Pebble Mill got to hear of the Thames Valley Horticultural Society's plans for a Barnsdale-inspired garden at Chelsea and decided that it would make a good feature for their programme, which goes out during the whole of Chelsea week, in the afternoon as well as the evening. The society had never been to Barnsdale and had based their ideas entirely on the videos and television programmes that Geoff presented. So the BBC invited four of them to come up and spent a day filming what they were proposing to do, interviewing not only the society's representatives but also Nick and Sue as well as filming all round the gardens and the nursery.

However, when the time came for the programme to be screened we all gathered round our sets in anticipation, heart rates rising and excitement mounting – and what happened? They didn't show it! I reckoned there would be a few members of the Thames Valley Horticultural Society who refused to pay the licence fee the next year. One of their representatives wrote to the BBC asking why such a good piece, in which they had all invested a lot of time, was not shown, but did not receive a reply.

Thames Valley Horticultural Society asked Nick and Sue to go down to Chelsea for a photo call, as did the Cottage Garden Society, whose courtyard garden was graced by *Viola* 'Barnsdale Gem'. Both photo calls were useful publicity for Barnsdale and Nick and Sue had a busy but productive day.

At the end of May the final shooting took place for another piece of publicity, a video that was being made about Barnsdale and what goes on in the gardens each month. Shooting had started last June and was now practically finished. The video was to be about an hour and a half long and would show all the gardens as they develop and the work that's done to maintain them as the year progresses, as well as the setting up of the show gardens at the NEC and the like. It was to be called *A Year at Geoff Hamilton's Barnsdale Gardens*. Next the editing, the voice-overs and the music would have to be done, after which it will proudly take its place for sale in the shop and elsewhere. It was a very expensive venture, costing around £30,000 to make, so several prayers were being said for its success.

~

Of course Nick and Sue are not able to spend all their time in the gardens and with the visitors. They have a multitude of other things to do, among the most demanding of which are the horticultural shows they attend.

The shows were now rearing their ugly heads and the activity in the show tunnels was frenetic. Though it is essential that plants are brought into bloom and look their very best for the shows, the judgement is a very fine one because one overblown bloom can spell the difference between a gold medal and no medal at all. So Sue spent practically all her time over the final weeks of May moving plants from tunnels with lights to tunnels without lights, moving plants outside in the shade or back into the light and warm, trying to slow them down or speed them up in a desperate effort to get them to flower at just the right time. Some of the tunnels had to be lined with shade netting because some of the more sensitive plants, like the hostas, had begun to suffer from the heat of the lights.

Nick was working on the show garden for the Gardeners' World Live exhibition at the NEC. This was to be a Compass Garden. Geoff always used to recite a mantra about the two imperatives for success with plants – good soil and the right position; and the garden was to illustrate the latter by showing plants that can be accommodated in each of the four positions in relation to the sun with a high chance of success. The garden was to have a centrepiece of a four-sided seat, each part shaped as north, south, east and west. Nick built a pattern for this in polystyrene before carefully cutting it out in wood. For somebody who failed woodwork at school he was very pleased with his achievement, as I think I would have been. His old dad would have been proud of him.

An entry for a show is always an exciting venture but the competition is exceedingly fierce, so although I had a good feeling about this one, whether it was likely to be a prizewinner no one would know until the day of the show.

The display garden at Gardeners' World Live won a silver medal for an innovative design

CHAPTER THREE

~

Great Expectations

~

June

Great Expectations

~ *June*

By June the gardens were beginning to repay all the hard work that had taken place during the wet and miserable winter and fulfil the promise of the previous months.

The big borders in Versailles were vibrant with colour and all the shrubs were clothed in their new summer outfits of bright greens, yellows and reds, like innocent children going off for their first day at secondary school in their new uniforms. The long, straight lawn looked lush and fresh, and the majestic urn at the end (which Geoff bought in lieu of a new suit) was planted up with a colourful display. The gracefully curving pergola that connects Versailles with the rest of the garden was now simply dripping with lovely yellow laburnum flowers, hanging in long, slender chains above the heads of the passers-by.

One day in June I made for the Woodland Walk. This was one of Geoff's favourite places, because it offers the peaceful pleasure of walking along a cloistered path bordered by ferns, grasses and woodland plants. It's a short stretch, but sufficiently long to furnish a better form of therapy than any of the psychologists in the world could offer. There is an uncanny feeling of calm and security here and, for me, a stronger sense of Geoff's presence than anywhere else in the garden. I go there often and it never fails to put proper perspective into any problems I may have.

ABOVE In the Woodland Garden the shoots of hostas, ferns and grasses gently unfold to greet the spring sunshine RIGHT The 'Hermitage', one of Geoff's favourite haunts, surrounded by *Dicentra* and other shade loving plants

And I always smile as I pass the Hermitage, a little hut, thatched with bundles of hazel, which Geoff built as a hide from which to watch the wildlife that abounds in this part of the garden. I smile because I remember that the BBC would never include it on any *Gardeners' World* programme, as the philistine producers thought that it looked too much like an outside lavatory. Once, though, a BBC crew – like many others, I'm afraid, signally lacking in good taste – set up an elaborate pretence of filming Geoff sitting in the Hermitage, and as he stepped out they played a recording, mischievously made minutes before in the house, of a lavatory flushing. It was several minutes before order was restored and the filming could begin again.

Just beyond the Woodland Walk is one of Geoff's favourite creations, the pond, stream and Bog Garden. The Bog Garden is linked to the pool and the water level is managed so that sufficient water overflows into the bog to maintain the plants in healthy condition. At this time of the year they looked at their very best, no doubt because of all the hard work and skilled attention they had received earlier in the year. The stream, with its bed of pebbles, gurgled laughingly into the pond and it was impossible to see that both are man-made: there was no sign of the butyl liner that covers the bed of each of these features and the stream seemed to come out of the vegetation as if it had burbled up from a spring. The pond is planted with water lilies, whose huge buds were just bursting into flower, while bulrushes stood

OPPOSITE Blanket weed must be regularly removed from the ponds to keep them alive and attractive

erect, as though on guard. Rushes and irises lined the edge of the pond and the surface was alive with water-boatmen skating effortlessly across the surface, while caddis-fly larvae, which build a protective cylinder of grit and leaf fragments around themselves, could also be seen by the observant eye. Frogs and toads gazed impassively from the undergrowth and, while it was a little too early for dragonflies, they would soon be seen swooping over the surface.

But it was the planting in the Bog Garden that was so impressive. It was dominated by a huge gunnera, called, by a happy coincidence, *Gunnera hamiltonii*. Although Geoff had quite a few plants named after him, this is not one of them – but if I know my brother the name was the reason he chose it. In fairness, he would also have been attracted by its enormous puckered leaves, which spread like a protective umbrella over the smaller plants. This giant architectural plant was set off by irises, with graceful, strap-like leaves and colourful flowers; astilbes, which have handsome pink or red panicles of flowers that keep their appeal even when brown and dry in winter; and hemerocallis, the day lily, the individual flowers of which are short-lived but follow on in abundance from June to September. The comely ligularia, a clump-forming plant with leathery, dark-green leaves that are almost mahogany on the underside, would bear large, daisy-like flower heads later in June, adding

a splash of bright yellow to the scene. As well as these and many other flowering plants there was a wonderful array of foliage plants – hostas, rheums and a whole range of rushes, sedges and ferns.

The Bog Garden is a place for contemplation and quiet. It is exquisitely beautiful and restful, even though underneath the calm exterior there lies a frantic busying of wildlife who have found the perfect environment for their survival and well-being.

~

The coffee-shop extension was finished in the nick of time. In fact Nick was assembling the new tables and chairs early on the morning of Pippa Greenwood's visit and had arranged them just as the first of the doughty band of visitors who were coming to meet her and listen to her gardening wisdom began to arrive. Brinkmanship at its very best.

The event was arranged through an organisation called Activity Superstore, a commercial outfit who set up all kinds of pursuits for active people of all ages – motor racing, surfing, rock climbing, canoeing, sightseeing and, of course, gardening. About twenty-five people attended, which was, in Pippa's view, just about the right number for her to be able to retain the personal touch that she is so good at.

Nick and Sue gave everyone a short welcoming talk and told them a little about the gardens, after which Pippa took them on a guided tour. Pippa knows the gardens very well because of her work with Geoff and understands why things have been done the way they have. She was also able to tell the group a few tales about the pleasures and the exigencies of working with him.

After lunch there was a short demonstration, centred mainly around the way to deal with containerised plants. Pippa had to borrow peat-free compost from Nick, because she had tried to buy some at a couple of garden centres on the journey up but found that none of them stocked it. Entertaining visions of Armageddon if she tried using peat-based compost at Barnsdale, she decided that discretion was the better part of valour.

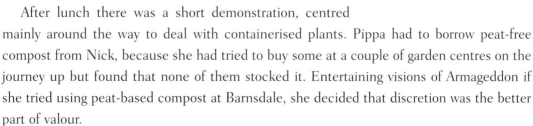

LEFT The little stream burbles contentedly past the primulas, ferns and other moisture-loving plants
ABOVE Geoff put his carpentry skills to good use in beautifying the garden

After the demonstration there was an opportunity for questions. Pippa, as most people will know, is a pest and disease specialist, so most of the questions were about her subject; the question of how to deal with slugs was thoroughly explored, as it always is on any *Gardeners' Question Time*, without ever coming to any serious conclusion except 'Learn to live with them'.

The visit was a great success and Nick subsequently heard from Activity Superstore, who said that they were very keen to repeat the event next year. The comments on their customer-satisfaction questionnaire distributed to all participants were all so positive that they had convinced them that such an event should become a permanent feature of their programme.

~

In early June Barnsdale entered the final phase of preparation for the first of the big shows, Gardeners' World Live at the NEC in Birmingham. There was an outward appearance of calm and efficiency, but underlying this was a feeling of tension and anxiety triggered by the fact that the Royal Horticultural Society's judging standards are so high that the slightest error of judgement in design or planting or a single blemished flower can dash hopes for a coveted medal.

The King Cup, *Caltha palustris plena*, graces the Bog Garden every spring. In more innocent times it would be strewn on the roofs of cottages to bring good luck

Last year the Barnsdale entry won a bronze, which was a disappointment, especially for Sue, who had given her all and felt convinced that she would do better. So this year there was a determination to beat that performance and to take another step in the long journey towards the ultimate gold and that greatest of all aspirations, Best in Show.

One of the problems that Nick and Sue face in this quest for success is that they lack the experience of some of the old-timers, which, by definition, can only come with age. Their collective knowledge of horticulture is great, as are their design skills, but these two commodities alone are not enough to win medals at the big shows. There is also a need to understand in the minutest detail what the judges are looking for; and that depends on who the judges are, a fact never disclosed before the show. The judging is done in camera, so there is no opportunity to explain the design or to overhear their conversation. So it is a process shrouded in mystery and dependent a lot on luck. If you are able to ring a bell with the judges you get a medal, but if not you go home empty-handed. Both Nick and Sue take every opportunity to seek out the old-timers and to pick their brains about weaknesses in their design, their planting and the quality of the plants themselves, and gradually they will gain experience.

LEFT The magnificent *Hosta* 'Frances Williams' is one of the most slug resistant varieties available
ABOVE Sue selling madly at the sales table at Gardeners' World Live

In the show polytunnels the hemerocallis and the salvias were close to perfection, so Sue moved them into the tunnel covered only with a fine netting, where the shady environment and maximum ventilation would slow down their development. Controlling the rate of development is a tricky job requiring the utmost vigilance, and Sue spent most evenings visiting her charges to check on their well-being. She also jealously guarded the job of watering and feeding, because the amount of water or feed each plant receives can have a dramatic effect on its progress as well as its health.

There is no automatic overhead watering system in the show polytunnels because the combination of droplets on the leaves or flowers and the strong glare of the sodium lights or the sun can leave blemishes that cannot be removed. So all the watering is done by hand. Watering is, in fact, a very exact science. If wilting occurs because of under-watering it is likely that the leaves will be damaged and the plant rendered useless for showing. Most plants will not thrive if over-watered, the effect being the same.

The problem is compounded by the fact that the show tunnels contain a wide variety of plants, all with different requirements. As if running a good restaurant, the maestro must know his or her customers and pander to their every whim. Some plants are non-drinkers, like the penstemons, hebes, lavenders, osteospermums and argyranthemums. But some are always thirsty, like lysimachias, astilbes, hostas and ligularias, and these must be placed on a plastic sheet so that they can retain as much water as possible and watched with an eagle eye by an ever-hovering waiter for the first sign of thirst. All this is made even more difficult by the condensation that forms inside the tunnels and drips on to the leaves, causing scorching when the sun comes out. A special close-meshed net has to be erected over the plants, to shed the water as it forms.

Two weeks before the show the plants were 'tidied up' by a band of patient ladies from the gardens and the nursery, who sat on boxes or folding chairs and painstakingly snipped out blemishes, removed any dead leaves, polished the leaves with leaf wipes to remove water marks and to give an added shine and, of course, dealt harshly with the slightest hint of a weed, admonishing them as they pulled them gently from the pot. Plants which they thought might not meet the exacting standards of the judges were replaced in the nursery for sale if good enough or, if not, discarded altogether.

During one of my visits I wandered in to one of the show tunnels and found Margaret, Dave's wife, Emma Porter, a student, and Joan Lakeland. All of them usually work in the nursery, but that day they were playing fairy godmother to a bunch of healthy and exuberant plants. Carefully snipping out blemishes and trimming round the edges of leaves to maintain a perfect leaf shape, they were ensuring that they could all go to the ball – and not like the ugly sisters but in resplendent glory, like Cinderella.

Emma had been working part-time at Barnsdale for about four years, during her vacations from Lincoln University where she was studying psychology. She would be staying at the show, accompanied by her boyfriend, Jon, the head gardener. They would stay in a caravan parked close to the site, to enable an early start each day. They liked this part of the job because it gave them an opportunity for five romantic evening meals in local restaurants, at the boss's expense – an experience to be savoured indeed.

My suggestion to Emma that her psychology talents may be of more value at Barnsdale than her horticultural talents was received with a shy smile, which I read as a sign of agreement, but I didn't pursue it. None of these three ladies have been formally trained and all have picked up their knowledge as they have gone along, but each of them has developed a dexterity and a skill with plants that any experienced gardener would be proud of. Joan puts it down to the fact that her son has a landscaping business and her daughter is studying horticulture, so it's 'in the family', and Margaret puts it down to the fact that she's married to Dave and has no option. 'What do you talk about in the evening?' I asked. 'Gardening,' came the predictable reply, and we all laughed about our common obsession.

On Saturday morning, the job of loading the big transit van and Sue's horse box began, in preparation for the journey to the NEC. First all the hardware was loaded – the ingenious tree seat that Nick had built, carefully protected so that no harm would befall what had

become his pride and joy; then all the wooden surrounds for the garden, bag upon bag of bark and gravel, and all the other tools and accoutrements that are required for what is a military-style operation.

The plants were left until the cool of the evening, so that they would only leave their comfortable quarters at the last possible moment. Loading them was hard, anxious work that had to be carried out with the utmost care, and all the members of the team were grateful when they were finally able to slip away to their homes for a short but well-earned rest. Even though the loading had gone without a hitch, Nick and

The van was heavily loaded for transporting plants and equipment to the Gardeners' World Live exhibition and driven gingerly up the motorway to Birmingham

Sue were still anxious. Ever since the nursery has been open, Barnsdale has received the attention of burglars on frequent occasions and any damage or theft of one of the vehicles would spell disaster.

However, at six o'clock on Sunday morning, Nick and Sue were relieved to see that the van and the horse box were still there. A final check on the plants confirmed that they were all still in good condition and raring to go. It took three hours to get to Birmingham, double the normal journey time, because of the weight of the vehicles and the fact that they were driven gingerly, so as to avoid the need for rapid braking or turning, which might have damaged the precious cargo. Nick and Sue spent all day installing the wooden surrounds, laying the gravel paths and unloading the plants, after which they came home.

There was another early start on Monday when a team of six – Nick, Sue, Dave, Oliver, Jon and Emma – set off again for Birmingham.

Their first job was to tidy up those plants that had been damaged in transit or simply looked less than perfect. While this was going on Sue began the planting. Planting is perhaps not the correct word to use, because the plants remain in their pots and are plunged into a bed of bark, to give a natural look, while retaining the status quo for the plant. Remove it from the pot and it will begin to suffer from lack of moisture and will tend to spread, but safe within its pot it has access to all the water it needs and remains in perfect condition.

The job of placing the plants requires a high degree of skill and a good knowledge of the requirements of the judges. Sue paid careful attention to this job because she knew that if

BELOW LEFT The stand at the Gardeners' World Live exhibition richly deserved the silver medal it was awarded by the RHS judges BELOW RIGHT Nick discovered that plant sales at the show were brisker than expected so it was all hands to the pumps

colours clashed, blemishes were apparent or the planting was too dense or too sparse the judges would mark her down. The reason for the award of a bronze medal last year was that a part of the garden had been underplanted, so this year she gave that potential problem special attention. I argued that winning a bronze medal against the kind of competition that exists at a show like this is a significant achievement, but after witnessing the jutting jaws and the shaking of heads I knew that my argument went unheard.

The four-sided seat was placed to look as though it had been built around a tree which sat in the middle of the garden. First the full-shade section was planted, then the semi-shade section, then the dappled-shade section and finally the full-sun section. The result was not only pleasing but also instructive, demonstrating which plants prefer which position on the points of the compass. It thus reflected the whole purpose of the gardens at Barnsdale, which is to enable people not only to experience a beautiful garden but also to learn, through simple observation, how to solve some of the problems that may have been plaguing them.

The judging is done as soon as the show opens, before any visitors are allowed into the marquee, so that visitors can see what kind of medal has been awarded to each exhibitor. While the judging is taking place, none of the exhibitors can be present either. A group of serious-faced experts visit each stand and inspect it with intense concentration while discussing its merits and failures. They then award the medals, placing a small plaque on each stand that has won one, and then the impatient hoards are let in. Most impatient of all, of course, are the exhibitors themselves, all anxious to see what they have received – or not received, as the case may be.

Nick and Sue were straining at the leash to get to see what the judges decision had been, but they restrained themselves, trying to look as nonchalant as they could, in case they were in for a disappointment. But no! There, nestling among the plants that Sue had so carefully arranged, was a plaque announcing the award of a silver medal. The smiles on the faces of the two protagonists stretched from one end of the marquee to the other. 'OK,' said Sue, 'bronze last year, silver this, silver gilt next year and gold the year after that.' And if I am right about her determination, she'll probably do it.

Nick and Sue, with the utmost coolness, then went back to Barnsdale to take care of their beloved gardens, leaving the stand in the more than capable hands of Paul, Emma and Jon, whose job was to sell plants from tables laid out around the stand. And sell plants they did, fast and furiously. The unique nature of the stand awakened an understanding in many of the visitors of the vital importance of planting the right plant in the right place, so there was a scramble to buy plants suitable for some difficult corner of the garden that had always been a problem. Many visitors remarked how useful the display had been; and, judging by the number of leaflets about Barnsdale that were taken, there was also a desire to see more of the innovative and instructional methods used there.

There were many congratulatory remarks about the garden, the most common of which was the view that it should have received a higher level of award than it did. But then these remarks came from enthusiastic amateurs rather than from the critical and discerning eyes of a panel of highly skilled judges. On the other hand, perhaps there is a lesson here for the judges. Maybe points *should* be allotted to gardens that simply appeal to the ordinary, enthusiastic gardeners who inhabit the show – they can be pretty discerning too.

I asked Sue if anybody had talked about Geoff. 'Oh my goodness,' she said, 'all the time, all the time. It was quite an inspiration to hear people eulogising about how good he was and how nobody could ever replace him.' He was obviously still well remembered and much loved, although one lady was overheard saying to her friend, 'Oh look, this is Barnsdale. Isn't that Alan Titchmarsh's place?' At which Sue leaped up and said, with righteous indignation raising her voice an octave, 'I beg your pardon. I'm afraid I can't have that!' and went on to explain the difference between Barnsdale and Barleywood. Oh well, I guess they're both good, so it's no disgrace to confuse the master and the apprentice.

Very enjoyable day. Keep up the good work for Geoff's sake! – Sandra and Peter Adders, Alton, Hants (up the road from Alan Titchmarsh!)

Once again Nick and Sue took the opportunity to gather ideas from the old-timers, who always seem ready to share their knowledge and experience. Among the more down-to-earth tips they received was one from one of their favourites, Jim Blythe, who has been gardening and showing all his life and helps to co-ordinate the work of organising the stall-holders for the RHS. Jim's tip was, like all the best ideas, simple but immensely effective. He pointed out that if all the plant prices were rounded up or down to the nearest fifty pence, the only change that would be needed on the stand would be one pound and fifty-pence coins. Blindingly obvious when you think about it, but Nick and Sue hadn't thought about it. The idea streamlined the selling operation so much that, while it was still hard work and rushed, the queues of people were much shorter than they had been the previous year, even though they were about ten per cent up on sales. Good old Jim! Incidentally I was interested to know if they rounded their prices up, as most retailers did during the memorable decimalisation saga, or down. Nick, with a look of outraged innocence told me, hand on heart, that they rounded them down. 'Very good value for money,' he said.

As the week went on the sales tables became busier and busier and every day saw the need for another overfilled vanload of plants to be shifted from the nursery up to Birmingham to replenish the stand. This meant a six o'clock start, so that the van could be unloaded at seven and the table restocked before another invasion by the hungry hordes began.

Though dark circles began to appear under eyes, nobody slackened for a moment. The feeling of excitement and success was electric and clearly stimulating to all the people who worked so hard and so valiantly on the stand. Every member of staff who could be spared from their duties at the gardens did a stint at the show, partly as a small reward for all the hard work they had done during the year and partly for the experience of participating in what was an exciting and challenging event. They all came home scourged by hard work but much more motivated and enthusiastic about what can sometimes be quite tedious work in the gardens.

At the end of the show most of the plants from the show gardens were sold. This is always a mad scramble that outdoes the January sales by far. All the plants in the gardens are perfect and considered a high prize by really enthusiastic gardeners. So as soon as the final hour of the show is signalled there is a rush for the plants which some people have eyed covetously for the entire duration of the show. It is not only the people who have come for the final day who are involved in this insane mêlée: many people come especially for the last hour, just to get plants that they have singled out during the earlier days of the show. If you travel home by train, as I did, you see the platforms crowded with people with huge trees and shrubs or weighed down with plastic bags full of exotic specimens, all facing the daunting task of manhandling their enormous loads through the inadequate doors of the train. It's a very amusing sight, which always convinces me not only that the train operators should provide cattle trucks for this journey but that enthusiastic gardeners are the most eccentric and lovable people in the whole world.

After the sale of plants, Nick and Sue, together with the exhausted staff, dismantled the stand and travelled back in motorised comfort, all looking back on an experience that was tiring, tense and very demanding but eventually exhilarating and satisfying, particularly as Sue clutched a silver medal to her breast as though it were a threatened child. It had been a good show for Barnsdale – but already they were discussing how their entry could be better next time.

~

There is, for me, a great beauty about the combination of discipline and informality that makes up a vegetable garden. Straight rows of plants, equally spaced, standing shoulder to shoulder like guardsmen, provide the discipline, but the splendour of their uniforms provides the informality.

On one lovely, sunny, optimistic day in the Allotment rows of bright-green spinach jostled with the shiny dark leaves of Swiss chard, standing to attention as if to show off the lovely white stripe down their trousers. A catch-crop of lettuce was growing into fat, white hearts between the two, while a little further down a bright-red lettuce was ostentatiously flying its own standard. Next were celeriac (to my mind one of the princes of vegetables) and carrots, still doing battle against the pernicious slug. Scorzonera and beetroot contrasted in adjacent rows, one with colour and the other with form, and Florence fennel, with its finely divided leaves and burgeoning bulbous stem, stood in superior isolation like a lady conscious of her own beauty.

But there were also failures and Dave is not too proud to leave these on display to the visitors. I know they appreciate this and are actually encouraged by the knowledge that even the best gardeners have their failures. In Dave's case there were several rows of carrots and parsnips that looked decidedly below par and were heading either for intensive care or for the attention of the Grim Reaper – probably in the form of slugs again.

OPPOSITE The allotment provides a plentiful supply of food crops during the year and is much admired by the visitors

But his brassicas were magnificent, much further advanced than I had expected they would be and seemingly unaffected by any pest or disease – as yet. I noticed the use of collars to deter cabbage-root fly and a covering of netting to keep off the birds, so it looked as if, provided he kept the rabbits away, he'd end up with a cracking crop.

Swedes, turnips and kohl rabi were just emerging, but the potato crop dwarfed them all. Row upon row of different varieties stretched seemingly endlessly along one side of the path. 'King Edward', 'Ratte', 'Maris Piper', 'International Kydney', 'Golden Wonder', 'Russet Burbank', 'Cara' and 'Desirée', to name but a few. Harvest time should be interesting. I made a mental note to remember to cadge a few of each variety from Dave, for tasting trials, so that I could compare them with the varieties I grow myself.

Next to the potatoes was a large bed of courgettes, marrows and squashes, all recently planted and all thriving. This was going to be a hugely productive garden this year; perhaps the terms of the Common Agricultural Policy would need to be reviewed in the light of a potato and courgette mountain rising up in Rutland.

On the day of the general election, I harvested the first crop of early potatoes in my own garden. This was a bit later than usual because of the cold weather, but never mind that – the great news was that Dave didn't have anything yet worth harvesting. Mine were delicious and we had enough from one root to serve for two meals, so I was well pleased. This meant that I retained the Lonsdale belt for early potato-growing and I think I can claim that Tony Blair was not the only person in the country to experience a landslide victory. Unlike Geoff, Dave would have no opportunity to tell people on television that he had won when he hadn't. I was determined to flaunt my superiority unashamedly.

My flaunting had to wait for a couple of days, but when I went to see Dave he had the good grace to allow me my moment of triumph and then concede victory, looking as deflated as William Hague had a couple of days before. Perhaps I should quit while I'm ahead and announce my retirement from the fierce heat of competition – but on the other hand . . .

That day Dave was suffering desperately from slugs. Poor old Dave. He's a martyr to his slugs. Half a row of the carrots that had been struggling on the previous week had gone and all his Florence fennel was now badly attacked. He had picked off what he could see and had covered the crop with fleece to help it to recover, but if it didn't he'd have to sow some more. I found it hard to resist telling him that my Florence fennel was flourishing – so hard in fact that I reluctantly gave in and gloated a little. Well, an old man has to pick up his pleasures where he can.

His experiment with laying wood ash between the rows didn't seem to have worked but the following week he was going to try another experiment for the HDRA, involving the use

of bran as a deterrent. He had to prepare two beds, each three feet square, and plant them up with lettuce, an enticing dish for slugs. One would be treated with bran and one would not. A report on the results would be sent to the HDRA, who would collate the findings of all the gardeners participating in the experiment and disseminate the results to all members at a later date.

'I see the mulberry tree is out,' said Dave, 'and that's a sure sign that we have had the last of the frosts, so I'm going to put out all my tender plants.'

'Do you really think the mulberry tree knows, Dave?' said I, ever sceptical.

'Oh, I'm sure it does,' he replied, and the conviction in his voice was such that I knew it was pointless to pursue my own belief that plants of any kind are unable to forecast the future – but then, I could be wrong. In my view the fact that summer was practically upon us was a much more likely reason why we should have had the last of the frosts, the mulberry tree was just responding to a bit more warmth. Never mind – I love Dave's curious beliefs and if they contribute to making a man as good to be with as Dave, who can argue against them?

~

In early June there was great excitement throughout Rutland when it was announced that the Queen would be visiting Oakham during Oakham Festival Week. Everyone immediately envisioned processions and bunting and little children lining the street waving Union Jacks, and there was even a veiled suggestion that the County Council would shake itself awake in its vast new palace, rub the sleep from its eyes and lumber into action.

Barnsdale went into a state of hyperactivity when Nick received a call from the Queen's Private Secretary, who announced that Her Majesty had expressed a wish to visit Barnsdale to see the gardens. It would be necessary, he said, for him to visit with a couple of officers from Special Branch to inspect for security problems and to prescribe the precise route the Queen and her entourage would take. A date and a time were fixed and the staff were briefed about the intended visit. The news brought a glint of patriotism into their eyes; backs were stiffened, ties were straightened and a determination was born to make this visit successful. Barnsdale suddenly became like the war room on the eve of the Battle of Britain.

On the appointed day Nick waited expectantly for the Private Secretary and Special Branch. The hour that had been arranged came and went, but Nick, understanding the inevitable delays that can occur with people of this rank, stood at his post close to the entrance. But then the next hour went by and there was still no sign of a private secretary or a policeman of any kind. Nick began to entertain doubts about the authenticity of the original telephone call and decided that it must all have been an unpleasant hoax. Of course, we don't know this, but it would hardly be professional to ring the Queen's Private Secretary and say, 'What the hell happened to you, then?' So we shall never know. Suffice it to say that there were a number of the staff who believed it was an authentic call and that nobody bothered to cancel the appointment. However, the Queen did visit Oakham – bunting was there in abundance, flags were waved and cheers rang round the town – but it could be that support for a republic has increased significantly among the more radical members of staff.

A notable visit that did take place was the annual excursion to Barnsdale by members of Geoff's favourite environmental charity, Plantlife, which is dedicated to the preservation of wildflowers and their habitats. Twenty to thirty very knowledgeable plantspeople and gardeners arrived in the afternoon and were given a guided tour by Lynda and Nick, which was followed by tea and a chance to buy plants and souvenirs. Lynda, now a vice-president of Plantlife, is very keen to promote and sustain the work which Geoff started and she does so with great style.

~

By now Nick and Sue seemed to have little need to supervise Jon in his new role as head gardener. Even Jon remarked on the fact that the job was a lot less stressful than he had thought it might be. Nevertheless he was glad to have the security of back-up from Nick and Sue when he needed it, the bonus of which was that their occasional consultations about problems helped him to increase his horticultural knowledge significantly. But his greatest relief was to find that the staff like and respect him. It can be difficult to move into a management position because one day you're 'one of the boys' and the next you're the governor, which often leads to resentment and difficulty. But Jon doesn't give in to the temptation to adopt an overbearing, authoritative attitude with his staff. He acts like the leader of a team, doing his bit when necessary and solving the problems of his staff as they come along.

The taller hedges present a challenge to the trimmer but they must still be cut with the utmost precision

Pruning all the roses in the gardens is a long and skilled job, which Jon carries out with the ease of a well-trained craftsman

Although the original plan was that each member of staff should have one or two gardens to look after, recently Jon had had a shortage of staff that meant that each person had up to six gardens to care for. However, two more students, both destined for Brooksby College after their period of experience, were about to start, which he hoped would ease the problem.

An added problem for him was that at this time of the year there is very little other than essential maintenance work to do in the garden – lawn-mowing, hedge-cutting, weeding, dead-heading and all the multitude of similar jobs, which never seem to be complete. Like painting the Forth Bridge, once the gardens have been weeded from end to end it is time to bend the already aching back and start again. So it's sometimes hard to motivate people to do what can be fairly tedious work. So Jon had to carefully juggle the more interesting jobs, so that everybody got their fair share – but he seemed to be succeeding admirably.

~

I received another e-mail, this time from Mrs Susan Rowe, who wrote:

Dear Tony,

I am presently reading your book Geoff Hamilton: The Complete Gardener *and thoroughly enjoying it. I was an avid follower of* Gardeners' World *when Geoff presented it and Friday evenings are not the same without him. I would just like to say how sorry and deeply saddened I was when Geoff died. Like many I felt I had lost a friend. Geoff always came across as such a lovely down-to-earth man who inspired my sister and me to go out and 'do'. We are both passionate about gardening and Geoff always made us feel that we could achieve wonders in the garden. I am currently starting a garden from scratch and bought your book to inspire me once more. I am reading it with great enthusiasm tinged with some sadness that someone like your brother is no longer here to reap the rewards of all his effort and hard work. Barnsdale is a wonderful, lasting tribute to Geoff and I am planning a visit this year.*

   Yours sincerely,

   Susan Rowe

Well, I'm a sucker for admirers of Geoff, so I replied, suggesting we meet at Barnsdale when she came up, which we did in mid-June. The gardens were looking at their loveliest. By the time I met Susan, her sister Michelle, her mum Meryl and her dad Brian, they had spent a few hours walking round and were euphoric about what Geoff had established and delighted that it was being so expertly and lovingly preserved and improved by Nick and Sue.

Brian was a vegetable man who had been in the habit of winning prizes from the time he was a small boy at school and, as a vegetable enthusiast myself, I warmed to him immediately. We swapped stories about the inferior nature of supermarket carrots, deciding that people without productive gardens had forgotten what fresh vegetables taste like, and various other stereotypically 'oldie' complaints, while his daughters looked on with benign and understanding smiles.

One of the points that Susan and Brian made was that while all the gardens at Barnsdale are mature and protected, their own gardens were mercilessly destroyed by their children who want only to play football, rugby and cricket on the lawn, doing untold damage to the plants in the process. I sympathised. My own kids were exactly the same. Brian and Meryl and I were in complete accord about the deep sigh of relief we breathed when they finally left home. Sorry, kids, I love you dearly, but the truth must be told. But we agreed that kids were just a little more valuable than plants – most of the time. Perhaps I'll suggest to Nick and Sue that they should design a child-proof garden and build it at Barnsdale. That would be a challenge.

What Susan and Michelle loved most about Barnsdale were not the hard-landscaping or the 'special effects' but the plants – the way they blend together in complete harmony to form little pockets of paradise. Geoff would have loved to hear this, because that was exactly his view about the garden: while the design is important it should always be subordinate to the planting. That's why he would have shrunk from appearing in *Ground Force*, which is ninety per cent about hard-landscaping and ten per cent about plants.

They found that one of the most pleasant parts of their garden tour was the fact that the television gardens had been maintained as they were when Geoff presented them, so reminding them of the things he had done and the pleasure they had got from seeing him do them at the time. Meryl said that seeing Geoff work at Barnsdale on television on *Gardeners' World* made her feel a part of it all, as though she was there, gardening with Geoff. If only she had offered her help earlier – I'm sure Geoff would have been delighted. She said that she felt his spirit was everywhere and that the whole garden was full of him, wherever you went.

They, like many others, were surprised at how small each of the separate gardens was. When they had appeared on television they looked much larger, but now they saw them 'in the flesh' they realised that each garden contained ideas and features that they could replicate at home. This, of course, was always Geoff's aim – to make gardens that fitted the size of patch most people had and to fit the depth of pocket that most people had. So while in the programme there were trips to stately homes, just to show gardening on a large scale, the essence of the garden and the overriding appeal for today's visitors is its division into small plots, similar in size to the humblest estate or town house, made to provide a little patch of paradise on a small budget.

Perhaps the most lasting impression this group carried away with them was just what can be done if you set your mind to it. They had all seen the picture of Barnsdale in my book *Geoff Hamilton: The Complete Gardener* as it was before it fell propitiously into Geoff's hands – a flat, uninteresting field populated only by tussocky grass, docks and thistles. And they had seen that it is now an interesting, floriferous, productive garden, filled with secret places and unexpected delights. Their tour seemed to renew their enthusiasm and determination to make something satisfying and rewarding, which would give them years of pleasure. Susan was effusive in her praise for Geoff and what he had done for her: 'I looked at the picture in the book and I could see Geoff standing there and saying, "There you are. It can be done!" And as I walked round I could see his mature plants and think, I've got that, and that, and that, and this is how they'll look in a few years' time. I think it's brilliant.'

They were fascinated to see the tunnel cloches made from lengths of alkathene water pipe – at this time of the year demonstrating their versatility by the fact that the water pipe was supporting netting to protect the brassicas from birds. They were pleased by the simplicity of Geoff's ideas because it meant that they were not daunted by the thought of erecting complex structures. Nor did Geoff suggest they should try cultivating difficult plants in difficult conditions. There was very little at Barnsdale, they felt, that they could not do themselves – except for some of the hard-landscaping. But I explained to them that if you do it as Geoff suggested at least you know that you are choosing the easiest way and, for the things that need a little more skill – paving, brickwork, stonemasonry and so on – you just have to keep trying. With practice it will come. He certainly taught me how to do all these things and I'm quite proud of mine. And I can tell you that if I can do it anybody can do it.

Could feel Geoff there in spirit.
– Liz and Stuart Campbell, Shipley

Susan said to me, 'Do you know what has left the biggest impact on me? Birds. Everywhere you go the air is filled with birdsong and you don't get that anywhere now, not even in the country. I can remember how when I was a little girl I would wake up to a tremendous orchestra of birds. But you don't hear that now.'

'That is because we have destroyed their food source and their habitat through the use of chemicals and intensive farming. Here at Barnsdale the gardens are entirely organic,' I replied, adopting a proprietorial tone, as though I owned the place. 'If you want birds, don't use chemicals – the two just don't mix. Here they have an abundance of food, plenty of water and a million nesting sites. It's like Butlins for them. No wonder they come.'

'What about slug pellets?' asked Susan.

'No chemicals are used here at all,' I said. 'If you use slug pellets you'll kill birds and small mammals. If your cat picks them up you'll have killed that as well. If you want a garden full of dead birds, hedgehogs, field mice and cats, slug pellets are the answer.'

A young visitor prepares to carry home a reminder of her parents and a happy day at Barnsdale

Although I perhaps exaggerated just a little, I think I made my point. But in any case perhaps Susan and her sister were just testing me because they both revealed that they had taken the advice in my book and each evening they go round their gardens picking up all the slugs and the bugs they can see and disposing of them. Well done, girls! Keep the organic flag flying.

It had been a terrific afternoon for me. I had thoroughly enjoyed speaking to a family who were so passionate about their gardens and it was a huge source of pride to me to think that it was my brother Geoff who had inspired their passion. I know they got a tremendous lift from their visit to the gardens and I had a sneaking suspicion that I'd be seeing them all again. I hope so. After the obligatory book-signing I was marched out to the gardens for a photograph with them all. Well, there's no accounting for taste. Then they decided to visit the nursery to buy some plants, not so much for the plants themselves but because they recognised that the vast majority of the nursery plants are grown from cuttings or seed from the gardens and they wanted to take back a little bit of Geoff. It's sometimes hard to keep a tear from the old and rheumy eye.

~

Wonderful. I really loved the Artisan's Cottage Garden. I did some paintings of it.

– Diane Cotterill, Leicester

At this time of the year the Artisan's Cottage Garden is full of flower and very beautiful. There is a real sense of ownership in this garden. Not ownership by a busy business setting out to serve the public, but ownership by an imagined working-class countryman who cherishes the sanctity and serenity of the tiny plot he considers himself lucky enough to have and who finds his satisfaction from working in it. Of course, in the not-too-distant past working-class people often had quite large gardens, which they needed to grow enough food to support their families, but the size of this garden mirrors the size of the average estate garden of today, so that people can be inspired to reproduce what they have seen in their own plot, regardless of where they live. This is part of the magic of Barnsdale. In each garden one gets the impression that it is actually speaking to you. It is so easy to become lost in imaginings of what it would be like to have a garden like this, or which parts you wish to take away with you to reproduce at No. 10 Railway Cuttings, or wherever you live.

This little garden was designed to show how a typical cottage gardener of old could manage on the often meagre wage that a job on the farm, in the mill or on the railway, for instance, would bring in. So it was designed to be cheap, with a lot of self-perpetuating plants and low-cost materials, to fit a small budget. Geoff considered it entirely relevant to modern needs, because there are, of course, a lot of people managing on a tight budget today, and also because it aligns with the yearning by many people to return to what seems to be the more tranquil life of yesteryear.

In mid-June it was ablaze with aquilegias, which self-seed readily, removing the need for

ABOVE Picking the massive crop of redcurrants is a pleasurable but mouth-watering job and the staff occasionally succumb to the temptation to sample the product RIGHT The broad beans are firmly staked to support a heavy crop, which will supply a delicious accompaniment to many meals from late summer onwards

visits to the seedsman or the garden centre; lupins with majestic erect stems, packed with flower; geraniums showing soft blue flowers, which spread and can easily be divided; superb, stately foxgloves, which also scatter seed for a new and bigger brood next year; and a commune of other plants, all living in peace and love beside one another. The little vegetable and fruit garden, composed of two small deep beds as well as cordon apples, fan-trained trees and soft fruit, would provide some of the basics to feed the family, though it was not big enough to make it self-sufficient, as the cottage gardens of old would have been. Now it was neatly planted with salad crops, carrots, beetroot and turnips, as befits the modern small garden, but in the so-called 'good old days' it would have been ten times the size and overflowing with all the 'fill-belly' crops needed to feed large families – potatoes, brassicas, swedes, turnips, peas, beans and dozens more.

Of course, none of Geoff's gardens would have been complete without some of his 'artefacts' and in this garden there is an artfully constructed tool chest and one of his trademark 'beehive' compost bins; the most typical of Geoff's structures is the arbour, which was now covered with sweet-smelling honeysuckle and clematis. Geoff was quite a spiritual man in his way, despite his fun-loving exterior, and he would almost always finish a garden with a place of repose, partly for 'admiring time' after his work in the garden and partly just to meditate on the beautiful environment that he and nature had constructed together.

The humble artisan has a toff living next door who has the Gentleman's Cottage Garden, designed in recognition of the fact that in these days of greater affluence some people are able to lash out a bit of their 'hard-earned' on the garden. So it is bounded by a sumptuous yew hedge, which invites a hand to run over its closely clipped surface. This, even today, is an expensive item, way beyond the range of the modern-day artisan but present in the gardens of many better-off owners. Inside, instead of the artisan's gravel paths there are mellow brick paths in the form of a cross, in the middle of which is a roundel of bricks finished in the centre by an guileful circle of terracotta flower pots fitting closely inside each other in ever-decreasing sizes. Box hedges line the paths, making a very attractive display in themselves.

Here again splendid lupins were blooming, causing one to speculate whether the artisan had nipped across in the night to pinch some of the seed. And why not? There were astrantia, not yet in flower but already promising a mass of delicate pale-pink flowers, born on long, stiff stems; and anthemis, the chamomile plant, which would contrast with daisy-like yellow flowers. Pride of place is given to the roses, which were a mass of breaking buds. Clematis

A beautiful and melancholy place. I can imagine Geoff here still.

– Claire Pelta, Stroud, Glos

LEFT The graceful flowers of *Lonicera periclymenum* 'Graham Thomas' is a splendid climber, despite its cumbersome name ABOVE The splendid Gentleman's Cottage Garden, with its elegant brick paths and love seat, is ablaze with colour for most of the year

This small circular lawn in the Ornamental Kitchen Garden is an interesting feature for any small garden

and roses climbed the trellis together, competing for attention, and close by, edging the small circular lawn, some exotic irises were displaying their orchid-like blooms. The sedums looked strong and healthy, set to provide a splash of deep red in autumn, their blue-grey leaves contrasting gently with the fragile blue flowers of geraniums.

The small herb garden in one corner of the garden is again divided by neatly clipped box hedges and each section contains a different herb. The first is lavender, which is said to cure swollen ankles, ease tension, relieve injuries and heat rash as well as making an antiseptic household cleaner, room freshener and face oil, not to mention keeping the fleas from your pets. In the second is hyssop to sweeten hot drinks; in the third is origanum, an aromatic herb used mainly for cooking but also as a treatment for sore throats and coughs, digestive upsets and toothache. My word, the gentleman who had this garden would have been fit and healthy!

Growing in surprising abundance in a tiny deep bed there were vegetables to sustain him: leeks, courgettes, carrots, beetroot, broad beans and some tempting lettuces, all soon to grace the lucky man's plate. His topiary was beginning to thicken up and take the shape of two proud birds, strutting motionless beside the path. Of course, no country gentleman in the nineteenth and early twentieth centuries would have had a garden so small, but the real purpose of this garden was to demonstrate that, with a little more expenditure, such a cottage garden could be produced, even on an estate-sized plot.

~

While all in the gardens burgeoned and flourished, there was a distressing event that demonstrated a potential difficulty that every organisation that is open to the public has to face up to. An elderly couple had been making their way from the west of the country to Norfolk for a holiday and they decided to stop at Barnsdale on the way: it had always been one of their ambitions to visit the gardens and this seemed a good opportunity. It was a blisteringly hot day and the walking must have been something of a strain, because they had not been in the gardens for more than twenty minutes before the gentleman collapsed and fell to the ground. Sue was alerted by radio and she hurried over with Richard White, the new weekend car-park attendant, who is a trained first-aider, to find that the gentleman was still breathing but ashen-faced and clearly very ill. By a cruel stroke of fate the electricity sub-station next to Barnsdale had gone down and the telephone was not working, so Anthony, one of the students, had to call for an ambulance on his mobile phone. But this connected with the mobile emergency service, who then had to alert the ambulance service, so there was some further delay. To make matters worse, the ambulance crew didn't know the whereabouts of the gardens, so they had to phone for directions. It took fifty minutes for the ambulance to arrive and during this time the poor man was slipping in and out of consciousness. When they arrived he was put on to a stretcher and rushed to hospital in Leicester.

Much to the relief of all the staff involved at Barnsdale, the gentleman's wife telephoned later from Leicester to say that he had stabilised and was once more looking forward to his holiday. Although he had been suffering from high blood-pressure, his problem had been nothing more than heat-stroke – but the potential seriousness of the incident had shaken everyone at Barnsdale.

This unfortunate incident prompted Nick and Sue to review their provisions for such emergencies and it was decided that, although it wouldn't have made any difference in this instance, it seemed to wise to have more staff qualified in first aid. It is a bizarre fact that the gardens have no responsibility to provide first-aid facilities for the visitors – only for the staff. So provided the area conforms to the requirements of the Health and Safety Executive it would seemingly be in order, if a visitor collapsed, for staff simply to walk by on the other

PREVIOUS PAGES, CLOCKWISE FROM TOP LEFT: *Polygonatum multiflorum,* or 'Solomon's seal' is a mass of poised arching stems, delicate white flowers and a scent which fills the garden; *Hypericum* 'Hidcote', promising a mass of large yellow flowers from mid-summer to early autumn; This beautiful geranium blends perfectly with the *Dicentra spectabilis* in the background; The clump-forming *Heuchera cylindrica* makes a bold statement in spring and will bear graceful spikes of small greenish-white flowers in summer; The lovely pea-like flowers of *Piptanthus laburnifolius* will grace the gardens through the spring and into summer; This fine display provides a charming foreground to the small bridge in the Woodland Walk

side. However, apart from being just a touch ignoble, that kind of behaviour is definitely not good for business. So about half the long-term staff were sent away on a course to learn at least the basics, so that there would always be somebody available to deal with an emergency if one should arise. Now there is a fully trained team of eight qualified first-aiders, so visitors can feel secure in the knowledge that they can be as ill as they wish and they will be well looked after.

~

While I was walking in the gardens on one of my endless, pleasurable perambulations, lost in thought like Winnie-the-Pooh, I was accosted, as I often am, by a couple who recognised me because of my likeness to Geoff. They were Trina McGilveray from London and her Dutch friend Lidi Groenendaal – names to conjure with. They had come to the gardens because they had read my book. I can't tell you how satisfying it was to discover both the people who had read my book. They had both been Geoff fans for many years even though they had each lived in Holland, Lidi permanently and Trina until recently. (It's amazing how Geoff's popularity seems to spread to the four corners of the earth. When Geoff was alive I was frequently recognised and mistaken for him when travelling abroad.)

Trina said, 'I've lived abroad for a number of years and the only way I could get my ration of Geoff Hamilton was to read the books, because we couldn't receive the programme. When he became organic I did the coir, I did the artificial stones, I didn't spray and all that sort of thing. It was very much the integrity that I was looking for in a gardener. When I moved to Holland I became friends with Lidi and we would read the books together. We could also get *Gardeners' World* on the television, so that's how Lidi learned about Geoff. Then when I subsequently moved back to London I asked Lidi to visit and I told her that I'd take her to Barnsdale. Well, as soon as she heard that she jumped on a boat and came across – and here we are.'

Then she said, 'You made me cry in the bath!'

'Oh,' said I, taken aback, 'how on earth did I make you cry in the bath? It's not a thing I've ever achieved before, at least, not over such a distance.'

Trina said, 'When I got your book I used to sit in my kitchen or in my garden on an old park bench I have, with some trellis over it and a hop growing through, and read a chapter a day, gathering ideas. When I got to the last chapter I felt compelled to finish the book, so I got myself into the bath, before getting into bed, and I just found it so moving. I thought about all the things he'd achieved and the close relationship that he'd had with you, which I didn't know about before, and I was overcome with a feeling of loss. There was never going to be anybody quite like Geoff and that is a sad, sad loss. This week we've been to Beth Chatto's garden near Colchester and we've been to Audley End and several other wonderful gardens, but Barnsdale is the crowning glory.' Geoff would have blushed to the soles of his feet if he'd heard that, but that big, generous grin would have spread all over his face and his pleasure would have been unmistakable.

Their favourite features were the Cottage Gardens, especially because they mixed flowers and vegetables and because of the ingenious paving patterns and shapes that had been created – the minute attention to detail demanded by a truly practical man serving those who didn't necessarily have huge gardens but still wanted to be surrounded by beauty. Once again, their greatest surprise, as so many others', was the small size of each of the gardens, which they said looked a lot bigger on television, giving them both the feeling of 'Hey, I can do this.' This, of course was just the kind of enthusiasm that Geoff was trying to generate – what he called the 'can-do' attitude – and it was such a pleasure for me to hear how well he had succeeded.

After leaving this amiable pair of gardening friends, I moved on. But I hadn't travelled more than another five yards down the path when I felt a hand on my shoulder and a man saying, 'Your brother saved my life.' Intrigued, and envisioning Geoff casting off his jacket to dive heroically into the icy depths, or dashing into a burning building with nothing but a wet handkerchief tied around his mouth, I wanted to know more.

The man concerned was Geoff Walton, who had been promising his wife Janet that they would soon visit the seat of what had been a remarkable conversion. His story was sad but triumphant and, to me, deeply moving.

An element of surprise round every corner. Magical and exciting. – Sue, Keith and Shea d'Arcy, Swindon, Wilts

Beloved TV series brought alive. Removed some weeds for you, Geoff!! – Margaret and Paul Hammond, Newcastle, Staffs

Geoff and Janet had, tragically, been delivered of a brain-damaged child, a son, and Geoff, clearly a very sensitive man, had lapsed into a deep depression as a result. He couldn't sleep, he lost weight, his job as a teacher began to suffer and finally he began to drink too much, to escape the horrors in his head. Then, one miraculous day, he happened to be slumped despondently in front of the television when *Gardeners' World* came on to the screen. There was this friendly face, smiling out at him, demonstrating something that could be done in the garden and saying, 'Come on, you can do this!' And Geoff suddenly realised that this was true. Here was something – gardening – that he could achieve and from which he could get the satisfaction and tranquillity he so desperately needed. He said to me, 'I'm a teacher and I recognised another one. Geoff was just a superb teacher and, like the very best teachers, he inspired me to go and try for myself.'

'And now,' said Janet, 'he's really got the bug. I can't keep him out of the garden.'

'What's more,' said Geoff, 'I now have a garden that I think I could transport to Barnsdale and Geoff would be proud of it. I think of him all the time in my garden. We've become the two Geoffs.' I would blush to tell you how this made me feel.

$$\sim$$

While the whole of Barnsdale is a joy for me to visit, there is one place to which I return whenever I go there – Geoff's Memorial Garden. It's just a small, quiet corner, as Geoff would have wished, and it revives good memories for me every time I visit it. The centrepiece is a bust of Geoff, mounted on a stone plinth and made by his youngest son, Chris, who is a potter and now, by an extraordinary coincidence, head of Art at Hertford Grammar School, the school that Geoff and I terrorised in our youth. It is actually called the Richard Hale School now, after its founder, because it has become one of the dreaded comprehensives, but I still refer to it as Hertford Grammar School, which Chris always patiently corrects. The bust is a superb piece of art and held in great affection by me, partly because, since it was made after Geoff's death, Chris asked me to sit for him on the occasions when he felt he hadn't got a feature exactly right. I must be the only surrogate model in the history of art.

The bust is surrounded by a bed of roses which in early June were not yet in flower but showing a multitude of buds, which promised a fitting tribute to a great gardener. Opposite the bust is a wooden bench of unusual design, made by Peter Wallace, a great friend of Geoff and mine, who has done a lot of beautiful woodwork in the garden and the house. Peter donated the bench and the rare hardwood timber was bought by the staff, in memory of Geoff. When visitors are in the gardens that seat is always occupied by people clearly moved by memories of Geoff and it is by no means unusual to see a tear on the occasional cheek. Behind the bench is a small wildflower meadow which was studded with ox-eye

In the Memorial Garden the unusual bench, made and donated by Peter Wallace, with timber donated by the Barnsdale staff, sits peacefully in the gentle splendour of the Wildflower Meadow

daisies, campion, poppies, red clover, buttercups and the like, making a natural backdrop to a place of great beauty for some and pathos for many.

Close by is the Reclaim Garden, designed by Adam Frost of Oakham, once Geoff's landscape gardener, which sets out to show how an attractive garden can be made from discarded materials. It would be wrong to suggest that because the materials were discarded they were necessarily cheap, because many of them were bought from demolition yards, from canny people who know the value of everything. For example, the pergola that spans the garden is constructed from huge oak beams which, though expensive, repay the garden with a truly wonderful feature. Now it was covered with cascading clematis, roses and honeysuckle, not all of which were in flower but which promised a sensational display in a month's time. At the front of the garden is a small fountain made in the shape of a rose and constructed from an old copper water cistern by Christian Funnel of Hove; while at the back of the garden stands a statue of a gardener, made from old mower parts by Peter Cockburn, who is not only a talented sculptor but can also work wonders with recalcitrant garden machinery. When it was originally designed it was a soldier, holding a spear, but Geoff, with his typical 'swords into ploughshares' approach, insisted that the spear should be made into a hoe and that the figure should look more like a gardener than a soldier.

This little garden is bounded by a Victorian railing fence, which was now almost hidden by roses, showing large and sumptuous buds; a glorious group of hostas, completely free of slugs; some *Dactylis glomerata* 'Variagata' or cock's foot, a stately grass with lovely variegated leaves; an array of campanula, with bell-shaped, papery blue and white flowers; and clumps of potentilla, showing off with rich, golden-yellow flowers – as well as many others. It was a sight to cause all but the most insensitive visitor to stop in their tracks and wonder at the beauty that can be created by man and nature working together.

Round the corner from this was the artificial rock garden that I was so scathing about when Geoff began his experiments to find a substitute for natural limestone, the extraction of which was despoiling some magnificent rock formations. I often come to this part of the garden to reassure myself that I was right, only to leave, on every

LEFT Tying in the roses in the Reclaim Garden is a job for a tall man and a set of step-ladders ABOVE This ingenious sculpture of a gardener started life as a soldier but was 'demobbed' and modified to pursue a more peaceful occupation in the Reclaim Garden, at Geoff's insistence

LEFT Conical conifers frame the entrance to the Reclaim Garden ABOVE Spring bulbs are an optimistic signal of a cheerful year to come – and who would have thought that the 'rocks' were handmade by Geoff to demonstrate that gardeners do not have to despoil our natural limestone pavements?

occasion, reassured that I was wrong – and badly wrong. It looked magnificent. The rocks themselves, which Geoff made of sand, cement and coir, with some added colouring, have now aged and are covered with lichens, which take away all sense of artificiality. If there was not a notice there telling visitors about the origin of the rocks, I doubt if any of them would question their dubious lineage. The rocks are interplanted with alpines, which were now in full bloom and would give a colourful display right through the summer. This little garden is a statement not only about the ingenuity of a very inventive man but also about his dedication to the preservation of the countryside and his stubborn determination not to be beaten by those who set out to profit at its expense.

CHAPTER FOUR

~

An
Unexpectedly
High Summer

~

July and August

An Unexpectedly High Summer

~ *July and August*

Summer was not a high summer in conventional terms. There were a couple of weeks at the beginning of July when the sun burned down as it used to do all summer long when we were kids – or so the story goes – but there were a lot of cold days and rain by the bucketful. This should have been very bad news for an open garden but, almost as though Geoff was sitting upstairs pulling their strings, the visitors continued to pour in. By early July, 27,500 visitors had come to the gardens – a rise of 10 per cent on last year.

This figure was not only because of Geoff's lasting popularity, although that was certainly the biggest factor, but also because of the publicity put in hand earlier in the year. Advertisements had been placed in the *Women's Institute Yearbook*, with tourist boards and in the journal of the Council for the Preservation of Rural England. Then there were special promotions in *BBC Gardeners' World Magazine*, *Good Housekeeping* and the *Daily Telegraph* magazine. Coach tours were organised, local radio stations were contacted; and there are special terms for HDRA members as well as RHS members. All the promotion was designed

ABOVE The many beech hedges in the gardens make fine architectural features, but only if trimmed regularly and carefully RIGHT Weeding is a repetitive job but it gives plenty of opportunity for thought and contemplation

to maintain the flow of visitors and to increase the popularity of a unique gardening experience. It had been a time-consuming and expensive undertaking, going on all through the year, but it seemed to be paying off. It appeared to have seen off the effects on admissions of foot-and-mouth disease, as well as the appalling weather in the spring.

The visitors are wonderful. It amazes me that there are so many people who share a common passion. They become deeply absorbed in what they see and it is not at all unusual to see people with pencils and notebooks jotting down the names of plants they fancy and even making sketches of features they would like to replicate in their own gardens. Inspiring people in this way to develop their own gardens is what Geoff dedicated his life to and he would have been like a dog with two tails to witness the fruits of his endeavours. It's such a pity that I am the only half of our partnership that can do so but I guess that's better than nothing.

When visitors recognise me as I walk round the gardens it's always a pleasure to share the joy they have derived from the garden and to tell them a little more about the real Geoff, but sometimes it throws up some amusing situations. I was walking past one of the many arbours that Geoff built, which now serve as resting places for tired legs, when an elderly couple sitting inside spotted the family resemblance.

'Excuse me,' the distinguished-looking gentleman said. 'Is it Nick who runs the gardens?'

'Yes, that's right,' said I, expecting to be asked to talk about Geoff.

'Oh right,' he said, 'and what about you – are you Nick's son?' Now this was an understandable mistake – after all, I am only some thirty years older than Nick – but I was prompted to go across and shake him by the hand. He had made my day. I hurried back to Nick to tell him the good news, but for some reason he didn't find it as heart-warming as I did.

It isn't always the case that people approach me, however. I often see them whispering to each other, 'That's Geoff Hamilton's brother,' as though I am some giant of a man whom they feel reticent about talking to. Perhaps I should make a placard to hang around my neck that says, 'I am not important and I like to talk about Geoff. I do not bite!'

When I was a mere stripling I used to pity people who worked in shops or banks or hotels, because they were forced to deal with what I then called 'The Great Unwashed British Public', whom I thought of as difficult and tiresome. As I began to meet more of them I modified that view. And ever since the gardens have been open I have changed my mind completely. Sure, some people can be awkward and unpleasant, but they are a tiny, tiny minority – particularly if they are gardeners.

Rained so hard but couldn't spoil 'our Geoff's' gardens. – Alice and Paul Fielder

The tiny minority are the people who simply don't understand that Barnsdale is a working garden, which is open seven days a week. It has always been a problem to explain to visitors that not everything can be done during the

Weeds that invade the gravel paths are regularly hoed out to maintain their pristine appearance

winter and it is essential to carry out some planting or hard-landscaping work in their midst. Of course maintenance work like weeding has to go on throughout the year. The lawns have to be mowed and the hedges cut while the visitors are present, which can, for a very short time, disturb the peace of a very tranquil setting, although every effort is made to do such work early or late in the day, when visitor numbers are lighter. When Nick explained this problem to one visitor he went so far as to suggest that he should erect some football-stadium floodlights, so that the work could be done at night. He may have been a keen football fan but he was clearly not a gardener.

But none of us who know Barnsdale well can begin to count the number of charming, interesting, unusual, courageous and side-splittingly funny people who we have met visiting Barnsdale and we all regard it as a daily privilege to have the opportunity to meet them. If only gardeners could get elected as a new political party I'm sure the world would be a better place to live in. There's a challenge, Titchmarsh. Get to it!

Maintenance work is a priority for the staff in high summer. It is not, perhaps, particularly exciting for them, although all of them would agree that it is better to spend your life surrounded by a beautiful garden than in a factory or an office. They all beavered away nobly at the task – which Jon rather prosaically calls 'clearing through'. It is obviously very important to keep on top of it. For example, quite apart from looking unprofessional and untidy, weeds can harbour disease and they extract water supplies from the soil, so it's vital to keep the soil as weed-free as possible.

A problem that has always existed in the management of the gardens is that the water pressure is extremely low. When Geoff was using the gardens only for television this did not matter so much, because he could confine his attention only to those gardens which were going to be used on *Gardeners' World*. He could just about get two sprinklers working, albeit at such a pathetically small output that he had to keep them going, in one spot, all night and move them to operate, again in one spot, for the whole of the following day. But once the gardens were opened to the public and they all had to look bright and fresh, the pressure was insufficient to water such a large area. So Nick had to install tanks and pumps so that he can collect

Remembering when gardening programmes were for real gardeners. Thanks to Geoff and family. – Chris and Paul Finch, Benfleet, Essex

water on wet days and distribute it over the whole area of the gardens when the weather is dry. Of course this is one job that has to be done when there are no visitors in the gardens. They have a tendency to complain when we pour gallons of water onto unsuspecting people.

~

I received a call from Ben Weston, a researcher from the religious affairs unit of the BBC, who asked if Lynda and I, together with Nick and Sue, would take part in an edition of *Songs of Praise*, which they would like to shoot at Barnsdale. It was to be a short piece, making up only a part of the programme, in which he would like Lynda and me to talk about the spiritual inspiration Geoff derived from his wonderful garden. Geoff was not a religious person, but he had a deep love of nature and a great respect for the plants and animals we live with that was for him a deep-seated spiritual conviction, so I said that I would be happy to do so and arranged for him to talk to us at Barnsdale.

When we met in July I showed him all round the gardens and he took lots of photographs of what he believed might be suitable locations. Enthusing prodigiously about the beauty of the place, he was obviously very keen to make a part of the programme there and he went away bubbling with *joie de vivre*, while Lynda and I began to think hard about what we could say during the short time we would have in front of the camera.

But then Nick got a telephone call to say that there had been a change of plan. Penelope Keith, who was rehearsing *Star Quality*, a Noël Coward play, at the Theatre Royal in Nottingham at the time, would now be presenting the programme and she would be doing

The charming little Italianate Courtyard Garden is a great attraction for visitors, particularly when resplendent with roses and herbaceous plants in high summer

the whole thing, so we wouldn't be needed. First we had been snubbed by the Queen and now by the BBC – I was beginning to think that nobody loved us. However, part of the programme was still to come from Barnsdale and they arranged to come along a week later to shoot the piece. It was scheduled to be a very brief snippet – a short piece to camera and a reading, and that would be it. They would arrive at five o'clock and be gone by half past.

Penelope Keith and her husband, who is also her manager, arrived at ten past five and it was good to discover that they were keen gardeners. Nick showed them round the nursery, they bought some plants and Nick gave them some *Penstemon* 'Geoff Hamilton' because they had been watchers of *Gardeners' World*. The crew arrived at half past five and they, the producer and Penelope were shown round by Nick, looking for the best location and the best light. During this amble round, Penelope told Nick about the new house she and her husband had bought in Scotland, which was to be landscaped by a local firm. The designer had suggested a water feature and Penelope, in her best *To the Manor Born* voice, said, 'A water feature? Why do I need a water feature? I'm only two hundred yards from the Murray Firth!' Well done, Penelope. That's the kind of gardener we like.

They shot the piece to camera in the Rose Garden and the reading in the *Daily Express* Cottage Garden, Penelope performing with the consummate professionalism that one can expect from a consummate professional. It all went very well indeed, although instead of the promised half an hour of shooting time it actually took three hours. The bonus attached to the overrun was that there was more time to talk to Penelope and her husband, both of whom turned out to be charming, funny and engaging people. Penelope, I realised, must be a good actress for she is not in the least as she portrays herself in most of the 'upper-crust' roles she has played. Geoff would have loved her. Penelope and her husband left with promises to return and the BBC crew just left – but we hope they will be back soon to take advantage of a most unusual and exotic location.

~

No sooner had things got back to normal after the Gardeners' World Live show than preparations began for the next big event, the Hampton Court Palace Flower Show. Hampton Court is a very different event to Gardeners' World Live, in that it is a gigantic operation, much bigger in terms of area even than Chelsea. It is mainly centred around the RHS floral marquee, which is filled with floral displays, special plant collections, plant breeders' exhibits and show gardens. Outside the marquee there is a vast assembly of stalls selling all kinds of garden equipment and household sundries as well as a 'plant mall', which contains hundreds of stalls where nurseries display and sell their wares. It was this part of the show that interested Nick and Sue, because not only is it a productive outlet for sales but it is also a very good advertisement for the gardens and the nursery.

Early on the first Sunday morning of July the trusty van and horse box were called once more into service, for loading. This was not quite as arduous as it was for Gardeners' World Live, because there was no show garden to assemble, so apart from a few ancillary items there were only plants to load. However, it was still a pretty tiring task, as the show requires a lot more plants because it is a bigger show and attracts a huge volume of human traffic – all voracious plant-hunters. The two vehicles were loaded up to the gunwales with plants, so that the springs creaked and squealed in agony. The last thing anyone wanted was to do battle with the dreaded A1 and M25 more than was strictly necessary: Hampton Court is a difficult place to get to from Rutland at the best of times, but when the show is on it seems

OPPOSITE Another arduous winter task is the cleaning of the huge water storage tanks, which will supply water for the gardens during dry spells in the summer ABOVE The actress Penelope Keith was warmly welcomed at Barnsdale when she came to present an edition of *Songs of Praise*

LEFT A dedicated seeker after plants cools off while examining the Barnsdale Gardens stand at the Hampton Court show OPPOSITE The display at the Hampton Court Show is designed for maximum impact to attract as many plant hunters as possible

that the whole world descends upon this already congested part of London. The plan was to set up on the Sunday, with as many of the plants as the two vehicles would accommodate, then to return on Monday with the remainder, so that only two trips would be needed.

The plants that are taken to Hampton Court are not show plants – they are mainly taken from the normal nursery stock. Nevertheless they are still excellent plants, which must stand up to the scrutiny of some very discerning and experienced gardeners. There is an awful lot of carrying to do, because the nursery stock cannot be depleted so much that there is nothing for the Barnsdale visitors to buy, so a lot has to be transported from the other nursery at Exton, half a mile up the road.

So there were some tired bodies about when the small convoy – led by Nick, driving the big Transit van, with Dave nervously navigating by his side and Sue following in the car, horsebox in tow – was ready to embark. Having reluctantly climbed out of bed on Monday morning, Nick and Sue returned to Barnsdale to begin loading the next batch of plants; but morale was lifted by an amusing little incident. Betty, the garden supervisor, has an aversion to technology (which is perhaps why she's such a very good gardener) so she prefers not to have to deal with the burglar alarms in the shop and the coffee shop. This problem is simply handled, because Nick deals with the alarms when he arrives at 8.30 each morning and Betty arrives at 8.45. But on this occasion Betty, filled with enthusiasm and a desire to be helpful on a busy morning, arrived at 8.25, before Nick. She barged into the shop and, of course, set off the alarm. Now, the alarm does not ring in the shop – it rings in the police station, alerting burly officers who run to their cars like RAF pilots scrambling to their planes during the Battle of Britain. As luck would have it, however, just as Betty went into the shop Nick arrived and, realising that he was about to be invaded by an irate cavalry, was able to phone the police to tell them it was a false alarm. A less than auspicious start to the day, which set Nick wondering if it was an omen for the rest of the day.

The journey to the show was the usual nightmare. We country people are just not used to the mad, scampering hordes rushing pell-mell to their desks, although a journey on the

M25 at that time in the morning can hardly be described as a rush – more of a gentle amble through carbon monoxide and road rage. Eventually, though, Sue, Nick and Dave arrived, and began to put the display stand together. As well as the display stand there were to be four trestle tables filled with plants.

Sue felt it was vital to set out one of the stalls with a display that blazed with colour, to attract the public. The plant mall is rather like a huge outdoor shopping-precinct, but in this case every 'shop' sells the same product. It's true that some stallholders specialise in particular species, but even so they are all selling plants and unless your stand can be differentiated from the rest you don't sell anything. So Sue set out to make her stand and stalls the brightest and most eye-catching of all. Whether or not she achieved that objective would only be confirmed by the volume of sales. Fortunately the Barnsdale stand was adjacent to a stand on one side selling only grasses and on the other to that of a specialist in fuchsias, so the Barnsdale stand would contrast with colourfulness and variety. A further stroke of luck was that the stand was positioned right opposite the exit from the pavilion and on the route to the plant crèche, where visitors can leave their precious plants in safety and security before returning to the fray to buy some more. It was perfectly placed to pick up the 'passing trade' and hopes were high.

After a very late finish and a long, long day, bad omens began to appear again when, just as Nick was driving off the A1, nearly home, the power steering on his car failed and suddenly the steering became so heavy that he almost had to get his feet on the steering wheel as well as his hands. He managed to drive home but he and Sue were filled with apprehension because Jon and Emma, who had agreed to stay down at the show each night to ensure an

ABOVE LEFT The stand at Hampton Court was constantly thronged with a press of people, laden with plastic bags, all looking for their horticultural heart's desire ABOVE RIGHT The choice of which plants to buy always presents a difficult decision for visitors

early start, needed Nick's car to tow the caravan to Hampton Court. So early the next morning Colin Eason, the owner of the local garage and a long-time friend, was called to do an urgent job to get the show on the road again. Colin, as always, turned up trumps and Jon and Emma were able to set off at about 1.30 p.m., arriving on the M25 just as the nightmare of the afternoon rush-hour was beginning. It's hard going, being a showman.

When the show opened on Tuesday the weather was fine and sunny and people poured through the gates. Sales on the Barnsdale stand were so brisk and the interest so high that they had to restock twice, which meant going all the way back to Barnsdale, but the journey was well worth the effort. Jim Blythe's advice about rounding the prices down to the nearest fifty pence or a pound was again put into practice and it made life on the sales tables a lot easier. When Jim visited towards the end of the show Sue gave him a 'Geoff Hamilton' rose, which was bred by David Austin Roses, to say thanks for the idea.

But on the final day of the show, Sunday, there was a lot of stock left. It had been hot and sunny for the first four days of the show but on Saturday the weather broke, rain began to fall and spirits were decidedly dampened. By Sunday, despite a positive weather forecast the show was drowned in a persistent, miserable drizzle. Very few people were about and those who were wanted to be inside rather than outside buying plants and getting wet.

Then at 4.30 p.m. came selling-off time – when stall-holders can dismantle their stalls and sell off their displays. Suddenly it was as if the Pied Piper had danced his way through the show followed by hundreds of avid gardeners and the stall was crammed with people, all eager to buy. The tables were practically emptied in an hour of frantic selling. From conversations with the other stallholders at the show Nick discovered that, while there had been a lot of visitors, people had seemed more reluctant to spend their money this year than they had last. But the takings on the Barnsdale stand were five per cent up on last year, so all in all it was adjudged to have been a roaring success.

By 9.30 p.m. the few remaining plants and all the accoutrements were loaded on to the van and Nick and Sue set off for home. They got to the slip road on the M25 and the traffic was solid. They finally made it to their home near Barnsdale by 12.30 a.m. A quick cup of tea, a brief exchange of views about the show and off to bed – utterly exhausted. At 2.30 a.m. the telephone rang. It was the police, saying that the alarm had gone off in the coffee shop, so Nick had to drag himself wearily out of bed, get dressed and go back to Barnsdale.

He was so tired that he could hardly see where he was going, but he eventually made it, only to find that the police had not arrived. He thought better of going in without the police, particularly in his weakened state, in case there was an intruder still on the premises, so he had to drive up and down until they arrived. When they did, he tried to open the door but found, in his befuddled state, that he couldn't do it. He explained why he was so tired, but the police said, 'Oh yes, sir,' and reached for the breathalyser. But just in time Nick got the door open – only to discover it was a false alarm!

~

The shop was now fully fitted and looking good, although there were some problems with the 'fully fitted' counter, which Nick described as 'the worst of British craftsmanship'. It made a lot of difference that nursery customers could now wheel their trolleys straight up to the counter, pay for their plants and wheel them straight out to their cars through the door on the other side. I held the old wooden shed that used to serve as the shop in great affection because it was like one of those improvised structures you find on allotments, but it was certainly a bit basic and difficult to keep clean and did not portray a very professional image.

The coffee-shop extension was also a big improvement. They say that when you build a new road it just attracts more traffic and the same seemed to happen with the coffee shop. It was always full before the extension, but now the capacity was more than doubled and it was still full – but we didn't ask where the people were coming from, just in case they decided to go away again.

A new kitchen was also under construction, so that the food wouldn't have to be cooked in front of the visitors and all the smells and sights of pots and pans could be hidden. It would make life for the coffee-shop staff a lot easier and enable them to deliver food much more quickly. While the coffee shop is not exactly a fast-food outlet, and serves only food that is fresh, wholesome and largely organic, it has to be recognised that the primary purpose of most of the visitors is to see the gardens, not to linger over a meal. When coach parties come in there is often a queue and, although this was minimised by pre-ordering, it remained a problem to be solved. Intercom between the counter and the kitchen would soon be installed so that orders could be relayed immediately, to try to ease the problem.

~

There was a sad day in mid-July when the bubbly, enthusiastic Susie Smith, who had started as an assistant in the shop and developed into a proficient gardener, decided she had to leave. She was in tears when she left, realising that she was moving from something inspiring to something dull and dreary, but she felt driven to leave. She left for financial reasons – her husband, who had been a manager with Tesco, had been the victim of one of the retail industry's periodic reorganisations ('downsizing' they euphemistically call it, when it should be called 'sacking people') and they had gone from a very good income to a fairly small one, derived only from Susie's part-time job and a much lower wage from the job that her husband had been able to get in a local factory. So Susie, with heart-breaking loyalty, went to work at the same factory to try to make up the difference. Well, at least they could cry on each other's shoulders during the lunch break.

OPPOSITE The dramatic yellow spikes of *Sinacalia tangutica* make a striking display from late spring to mid summer

In contrast, there was excitement for another member of staff. Oliver's old school had booked a visit to the gardens. The headmaster had asked if Oliver, the lad with the alleged speech difficulties, could deliver a short talk to the children before they toured the gardens, telling them about his job. This wise head had seen that Oliver would represent a good role model for the kids, demonstrating what could be achieved with hard work and application.

The headmaster had made a point of asking for a *short* talk, knowing that the attention span of his pupils would be brief, at which Nick had laughed and said, 'Look, there is no way Oliver can deliver a short talk. If you saw the way he'd overcome his difficulties and how the words just spill out of him you would realise that you're asking the impossible.' Oliver was clearly filled with pleasure when Nick asked him if he could lead the conducted tour. He is proud of what he does and how far he has progressed and, in my opinion, for what it's worth, he jolly well deserves to be – and so do the staff at his school.

When the school arrived, Oliver performed like a true professional and, despite Nick's declaration that it was impossible, delivered a short talk that really was short, the pride almost bursting out of his chest. He then showed the pupils around, talking them through the purpose of each garden and how it had been built and maintained.

A week or so later Brooksby College rang to ask if they could bring a party of Japanese students, with an interpreter, to see the gardens. Oliver knew the lecturer who was accompanying the party, because he had been taught by him, so who better to conduct the tour? Once again, he rose to the occasion and performed like a trouper. Oliver seemed to grow just a little taller during July.

A sizeable disappointment arose when Andrew, who had been at Barnsdale for only six weeks, decided he had to leave. Andrew was a university student, reading Media Studies, who had badly flunked his first-year exams and decided that he would pursue a career in horticulture as an alternative. At least he thought he had badly flunked his exams. He was thoroughly enjoying the work, and was doing very well at it, and Nick saw a bright future for him and was full of encouragement. But then his results came through and he discovered that he hadn't flunked his exams at all. In fact he had done rather well. So he decided to return to university. So Barnsdale lost a really promising worker and the university gained an inveterate pessimist.

$$\sim$$

One day I strolled over the bridge into the television gardens and came across Dave and Oliver, who were busy giving the trees on the fruit arch their summer pruning. The fruit arch was another of Geoff's stunning design ideas. It is a metal arch, about twenty yards long, with uprights about every yard, on each of which is trained an apple tree. The trees had put on some good growth and the whole arch was now clothed in a mass of leaf. In the summer and autumn the fruit, which is generally prolific, hangs in clusters above the heads of the visitors and jostles for space along the sides of the arch.

An urgent job to be done here now was fruit-thinning. There was so much fruit that it was breaking the branches, and this applied to almost all the fruit in the gardens – gooseberries, apples, pears, plums and cherries were all bursting to outdo one another. It seemed as though Mother Nature was compensating for her misdemeanours of the previous year. Dave had taken home four bags of under-ripe gooseberries, which he steams and presses to collect the juice. The juice contains pectin, which is apparently lacking in the strawberries from which he makes a gigantic supply of strawberry jam. Nobody could eat all the jam Dave makes, unless the whole family live exclusively on nothing but strawberry jam. He just can't bring himself to throw produce away. He believes that Nature has provided it so Nature should be respected and it should be put to good use. I fancied he'd be polishing his boots with it before the year was out.

Dave told me as he worked on the apple arch that he had ordered some pre-treated potato seed for autumn planting, which he intended to dig on New Year's Day, so that he could claim to have beaten me in the Great Potato Race. This seed is held back by storage in cold conditions, so that they are just chitting by the time they are planted, and the seed merchants claim that they will yield well. I wasn't sure that the use of pre-treated seed was within the rules and I said I would have to consult the International Potato Race Commission in Geneva before I agreed to take on this challenge. (But I have to admit that later I went straight home and ordered some of the same seed myself. I wasn't going to be outdone: I would dig mine on New Year's Eve.)

Paradise on Earth.

– Pat and Jim Bonsor, Longford, Beds

Still pruning, Dave turned to Oliver, who was holding the ladder for him, and said, 'And what about those cauliflowers we picked this week, Oliver?' He spread his hands about two feet apart, like the apocryphal fisherman. 'Big as footballs, they were!'

'Dave,' said I, 'that's bigger than a football.'

'Well,' he said sheepishly, 'a big football. In any case, we had a hard job getting them into a carrier bag. And the week before, when I was bending the leaves over I had to use a pair of secateurs.'

'OK,' I reluctantly conceded, 'you grow better cauliflowers than I do. But watch out – I'm working on it!'

Dave told me about his plans for next year. He was already working out what he would sow. He does this with the help of his faithful diary, where he records not only the crops that were sown but also their yields and resistance to pests and diseases. Such a record is important for the dedicated gardener, both in the vegetable and the flower garden. It enables Dave to decide which varieties don't suit the conditions prevailing at Barnsdale. The 'Winston' early potatoes he had dug, for instance, had had a good yield and were big potatoes, 'but,' he said, 'the slugs love them, so we won't be growing them next year. "Vanessa", which were grown on the same plot, were hardly touched.' With a good idea of what does well in the gardens now, he was going to reduce the number of varieties he grew and concentrate only on those that thrive. This would give him a little more space for the crops that do well.

He had also decided that he wanted to make the specialist gardens more specialist, particularly the Elizabethan Garden. Next year this would contain only the kind of vegetables that the Elizabethans grew. The actual varieties might not be available but he reckoned that, with a bit of historical research and the invaluable help of the HDRA, he would be able to

get it a lot closer to an authentic Elizabethan Garden than it was at present. The garden is laid out as a parterre, with deep beds surrounded by gravel paths, a true representation of the Elizabethan style and a great way for somebody with a small garden to provide succulent vegetables for all the family at very little cost. It is also an excellent way for the small gardener to keep control of the rotation plan. As long as there are at least four beds it is simple to rotate different kinds of crops around them, giving each bed a three-year rest and thus avoiding the build-up of pests and diseases.

Dave also planned to make this a 'no-dig' garden. As soon as the crops were harvested from each bed, he would break up the soil with a three-pronged cultivator, spread leaf mould on the soil and finally cover with a layer of compost. This would be repeated year after year, thus building a finely structured, humus-rich soil, which would only need the cultivator drawn through it each year. It would enable visiting wives to cruelly taunt their husbands about their previously solid excuse that they suffer from back-pain and are thus unable to grow vegetables. This should be an interesting development. The HDRA reckon that 'no-digging' is a perfectly workable way to run a vegetable garden; but, as a traditional gardener, who likes to see the soil broken down by frost, pest infestation reduced in

The sandstone pavement is home to this delectable *Saxifraga stansfieldii* as well as a host of other alpines

cold weather, plenty of organic matter introduced to the lower layers of soil and drainage maintained, I have my doubts. I will, of course, as ever, keep an entirely open mind and resist the ever-present temptation to taunt Dave if it goes wrong.

Dave was concerned that some of the vegetables in the small gardens – the Ornamental Kitchen Garden, the Artisan's and the Gentleman's Cottage Gardens and the Parterre Garden – had been less than impressive this year. He thought that this was because, while the flowering plants had been carefully chosen to suit the prevailing conditions, the vegetables had suffered from the lack of sunlight in these gardens. So next year he intended to try crops that have a longer growing season and are not quite so sensitive to low light levels.

Dave was about to go away on holiday, but he had organised it to fit in with his spraying schedule. The only spraying that is done in the gardens is done on the Allotment, and is of course organic. Every fortnight Dave sprays with *Bacillus thuringiensis*, which is a bacterial spray that feeds off the eggs and the larvae of the cabbage white butterfly but does not infect any other insect. This ensures that his brassicas look bright and clean and that the friendly insects are as well cared for as Dave would earnestly wish, and he wasn't going to let his holiday interfere with this schedule. 'I can then go away happy in the knowledge that my babies will be OK,' he said. I exploded at this. 'Babies, Dave, babies! These are a few cabbages you're talking about.' He smiled at me – the smile of a man happy with his lot.

He told me that his real pride and joy this year was compost. He claimed, just as Geoff used to, that it was good enough to eat. His only secret, he said, is that he cuts the raw material up very small with his knife before putting it in the bin, and then he turns it every three weeks. That's dedication for you. 'I'd like to turn it every two weeks,' he said, 'but I just don't get the time.'

He confessed, however, that he was not so pleased with his sweet peas. Since I had seen them in May, when they looked magnificent, they had been completely destroyed by greenfly, which proved impossible to eradicate by organic means. This sometimes happens to organic gardeners. When the weather and the atmospheric conditions are just right for the pest the predators just can't keep up; supply outstrips demand and the crop suffers. So what can the dedicated organic gardener do? Grin and bear it, hoping for a better deal next year. My advice is to sit and listen to the birds and the insects you wouldn't otherwise have and, one by one, count your privileges.

While we chatted over the pruning, Oliver told me, with great pride, that he had been accepted by Brooksby College for the National Diploma in Horticulture course, which he'd start immediately after his City and Guilds course. This, remember, was the boy who was reported to have speech difficulties. I can't say how delighted I was to hear that having battled and worked to overcome his problems he now appeared to have a fulfilling career ahead of him. If that's what gardening can do for a man, it has to be good. I pointed out that when he passes he'll have letters after his name and then he'll be able to thumb his nose at Dave. 'He does that anyway, the little blighter,' said Dave, his affection and pride in his protégé only too clear to see.

I was just about to leave Dave and Oliver when my competitive ears pricked up. Dave was saying in mournful tones, 'Ah, but my pumpkins have been a great disappointment to me this year.' It was almost as though he was the lord of the manor speaking about a dissolute son who had run off with the local barmaid. 'I've had to thin the fruits out to one per plant this year because they have grown so slowly. I may have to disappoint Wills and Harriet [Sue's kids] at Hallowe'en this year.' Oh, woe is me, I thought. If only I had those kind of problems. I worry about over-enthusiastic bank managers and the predacious taxman, and all Dave has to worry about is his pumpkins. Perhaps he has just hit on the secret of life. But at least I was able to announce that my pumpkins were thriving and my grandchildren were already measuring them up on a regular basis.

I left Dave and Oliver, really envying their opportunity to work in the garden full time. I just get the weekends for gardening and it is a mad rush from Saturday morning to Sunday night, with the constant frustration of not having enough time to make as good a job as I'd like. But even so, as I lie soaking in my bath after my exertions, gin and tonic in one hand and gin and tonic in the other hand, the sense of satisfaction is enormous.

~

One August afternoon I came across two schoolkids who were walking around Barnsdale; well, they were now retired schoolkids, but they had known each other all their lives, having sat next to each other at school and kept in contact ever since, despite moving to different ends of the country. Lorna Pickstock and Eileen Knowles looked and sounded like life-long friends and, if they will forgive my impudence, still had a good deal of schoolkid fun and laughter in their voices. They were gallantly escorted by the Reverend Clifford Knowles, looking every inch the retired reverend from an Agatha Christie novel. I enthused with him about vicarship, because I have always thought I'd have made a good vicar myself – riding round the village with a basket on the front of my bicycle, stopping only to have tea with the old ladies of the parish. He quickly disillusioned me, telling me that being a vicar isn't like that any more.

What was so engaging about these three was their bubbling enthusiasm for what they had seen. Lorna said that, while she wasn't a very good gardener herself, Eileen knew the name of every plant in the garden. 'But now,' she said, 'I feel inspired. I'm going to go home and I'm really going to get gardening properly. One of the things I've seen is that you don't let plants grow into huge clumps; you lift them and divide them. I just let mine grow and grow, so I don't get any flowers. Now I shall go home and divide them and I shall get some flowers next year.'

'And I've seen some great new ideas as well,' said Eileen, 'like sweet peas growing up the pergola. I'd never thought of that and it's so simple and so brilliant.'

I'd love to have spent more time with them but it was by then nearly five o'clock and they were desperate for a cup of tea, so I reluctantly let them go, with their promises to come back ringing in my ears.

~

August is a cruel month, despite the golden sunshine and the drier weather, because as plants are cut back or lose their will to flower the garden can begin to look tired and dull. But this is never the case at Barnsdale. One of the perpetual challenges of running an open garden is to ensure that, whatever the weather throws at it, it always looks fresh and bright, much as it did in spring. Of course, just like all other gardens, the spring and early-summer flowers were now over, but cunning planting and careful colour combination ensured that as one stalwart declined another stepped up to take its place. Many gardeners add to this colour with pot-grown plants which they have held back in reserve to plug the gaps as annual or biennial planting is removed or perennial plants cut back after flowering. But shortage of space at Barnsdale makes this impossible, so some very careful thought goes into the planting plan to make certain that a succession is achieved.

An example of how successful Barnsdale is at maintaining colour into high summer is a border at the approach to the little bridge leading into Geoff's television gardens, which I think is one of the most beautiful in the whole garden. It is a great, curving sweep of herbaceous plants and shrubs, and in August it was full of radiant colour and impressive architectural shapes. Bright-scarlet *Crocosmia fucata* 'Late Lucifer' was competing for attention with the tiny *Potentilla* 'Gibson's Scarlet', now a galaxy of starry flowers. Both plants were set off against a background of delicate green *Alchemilla mollis* and the pale-grey foliage of *Achillea filipendulina* 'Cloth of Gold', which was topped with dazzling yellow flower heads. More yellow brightened up the border in the form of *Anthemis tinctora* 'Kelwayi', with a cloud of daisy-like flowers born singly above a base of crinkled, fern-like leaves and intermingling with the blazing red of *Penstemon* 'Cherry'. All this part of the border

For a couple of anoraks this is the best garden we have visited – and we've been to some gardens.

– Mark and Julie Hedges, Skipton, Yorks

contrasted with the deep red of *Berberis thunbergii* 'Rose Glow', which provided a rich, almost aristocratic backdrop. *Miscanthus sacchariflorus* lived comfortably alongside a tall, stately acanthus, which has sharply divided, thistle-like leaves and bore many spikes of funnel-shaped mauve and white flowers which, thanks to the organic policy pursued in the gardens, were being fiercely attacked for their pollen by squadrons of insects of all kinds, filling the air with a gentle buzz. Next to that were astilbes, holding aloft banners of pale-pink panicles, splendidly alliterative and stunningly beautiful. Their next-door-neighbours were a clump of hydrangeas complementing their friends with delicate pale-pink flowers and, on the other side, some bergenias which have flowers of a deeper shade of pink, offset with large, spoon-shaped, pale-green leaves. The pink theme was completed with a backing provided by a lovely *Geranium asphodeloides* standing proudly but demurely, like a young woman at the edge of the ballroom floor.

The policy of all-the-year-round colour is rigorously pursued by Nick and Sue, for they see it as imperative that the visitors have something interesting to see whatever time of the year they come. And there are some familiar faces among the visitors – people who return time and time again, to note what is flowering, how it blends with its neighbours and what position it finds most agreeable, so that they can buy the appropriate plants in the nursery and make an all-the-year-round garden for themselves. Geoff always believed that the best way to teach something was to get people to do it and by inspiring people in this way this is exactly what the gardens have achieved.

As the month of August moved on new plants came into flower around the garden, to brighten and gladden the eye. By mid-August the cheerful phlox was in flower, as was the physostegia, the 'obedient plant' – so called because its flowers remain in place after it has been moved. Though obedient there was no humility in this plant as it showed off its lovely spikes of tubular dark-lilac flowers, as though conscious of its own beauty. While the tea roses were beginning to fade, the old English roses were really coming into their own. I'm proud to say that *Rosa* 'Geoff Hamilton' was now an absolute riot of pale-pink blossom. Sunflowers and helianthus provided ostentatious splashes of rich colour, while the faithful penstemons and tender perennials such as osteospermums and argyranthemum (until recently called *Chrysanthemum frutescens*) continued to flower their hearts out.

It takes a lot of care and skill to arrange a successional flowering and I can well remember asking Geoff the secret for a run-of-the-mill gardener like me, who was not so familiar with plant names and characteristics. His advice was to keep it very simple. Just go down to a good garden centre once a month and buy plants that are already in flower, making sure that you have the correct position and soil type for it. After a year you will have a garden that is guaranteed to flower every month, except perhaps in the darkest and dreariest of winters. Obvious really, but it just showed what a clever old cock our Geoff was.

CHAPTER FIVE

~

Mists and Mellow Fruitfulness

~

September and October

Mists and Mellow Fruitfulness

~ September and October

A fine, bright spell of weather marked the beginning of September and it looked as though what had turned into a reasonable summer would go on for ever. It didn't, of course, but while the dry, sunny weather persisted spirits were high and the work seemed easier.

Nick and Sue returned from a holiday in the Canary Islands (how the rich live, eh?), looking tanned, rested and ready for the fray. Their first job was to talk to Jon about the ornamental gardens, Dave 1 about the vegetable gardens and Dave 2 about the nursery. They were half-expecting to listen to a litany of disasters and complaints, only to be reassured that there had been none. They were perhaps slightly disappointed to find that the show could go on just as well without them, but that's every manager's feeling after a return from absence.

In the garden the collection of seed had begun. This is labour-intensive, but it is really done for two reasons. The first is that the seed is then known to be fresh. There are, of course, statutory controls on the preparation of seed but it is well known that some old seed is still released on to the market, bypassing the tests for germination rates because there is such a high volume of seed consumption that by no means all of it can be tested. The second reason for collecting seed is that most of the plants grown in the gardens or sold in the

ABOVE Dave the Druid lifts his potatoes by the light of the full moon, to ensure, he believes, an abundant crop and a grateful earth RIGHT A late crop of potatoes is covered with newspaper and horticultural fleece to force them on for a delicious Christmas dinner

nursery are rare or unusual and thus often difficult to obtain; and seed merchants selling such seed will often put only four or five seeds into a packet, which may cost £1.50. So it's much more economical to collect seed from the rare plants already established in the gardens. Seed for varieties not yet grown at Barnsdale is still bought, but this will gradually diminish as the gardens continue to expand.

The plants in the pond had to be thinned this month because Geoff, in his quest for a good television spectacle, tended to overplant with vigorously growing plants. Of course this is fine when you have to make an instant effect, but it can't be regarded as a permanent policy. It makes one wonder what the 'makeover' gardens that are now so popular on television and are often similarly overplanted will look like in a few years' time.

Another interesting thing I noticed at the beginning of September was that patches of green manure were starting into vigorous growth on the Allotment. I asked Nick why, when

he was practically fully immersed in muck and compost, did he bother with green manure. The answer was that it adds plentiful supplies of nutrients back into the soil and, for people without access to muck or sufficient compost, it is a good way of solving the problem of soil fertility organically. A chip off the old block, he wanted to show visitors how it can be done.

The Allotment was looking really good, with just about enough food ready to harvest to feed the nation. I did, however, manage a cruel smile when I noticed that the late potatoes, planted in a crafty attempt to harvest ahead of mine, had suffered an attack of blight and Dave had had to cut off the haulm to prevent the fungus infecting the tubers. Since I followed his sly lead and my crop was still healthy, I hoped to humiliate him again. That would bring an old man a lot of pleasure.

Another of Dave's disappointments was the result of the HDRA experiment he had done to test the effect of garlic as a deterrent against aphids. At the end of the experiment the pot containing the garlic had if anything a heavier infestation than the one without. The HDRA told me that the experiment had been inconclusive throughout, with some members reporting an effect, as many reporting no effect and a lucky few having no infestation anywhere in their greenhouses.

Dave's experiments with bran to deter slugs had also been a failure, as most experiments with these little varmints are. This was largely because of the fact that the bran simply got washed away by the heavy rain, so the results were totally inconclusive. Next year he planned to bulk up the bran with sand to see if that would work. But this kind of disappointment will not deter the doughty band of organic gardeners. They will just buckle down and keep trying until they find an answer.

~

When Nick and Sue were walking round Gardeners' World Live back in June they were approached by Martin Fish and John Stirland, who present *Up the Garden Path*, a two-minute gardening slot on *East Midlands Today*, our local BBC Television news programme. They asked if they could do a piece from Barnsdale, to which they received an enthusiastic 'yes'. They then said that they would like to do it around 4 August, to link in with the anniversary of Geoff's death, but Nick and Sue were due to be on holiday then so they suggested early September.

In the event the team arrived late because they had spent half an hour with their boss trying to get an extra thirty seconds of screen time, which they eventually achieved. The intricacies of BBC planning are sometimes a deep mystery to ordinary, rational people. The programme normally has a rather flippant style but Nick explained that they were serious about horticulture and didn't want do anything that could be seen to be demeaning. The

Dave is happy harvesting Swiss Chard

piece turned out very well indeed and was broadcast the following evening. They interviewed Sue in the Japanese Garden and Nick in the Knot Garden and they also included a clip of Geoff, so all in all it was a very nice piece of publicity for the gardens.

With planning beginning for next year, Nick was once again suffering sleepless nights as Sue, excited by a new idea, woke him with shouts of 'Hey Nick, what do you think of this?' The RHS send out the application forms for the next year's Gardeners' World Live and Hampton Court shows, which have to include details of the design, about two weeks before the acceptance date, so there is always a mad scramble to put a design together. Creativity of this sort is not at its best under such pressure and they were searching for suitable ideas in time for the deadline.

They had decided not to go to the Tatton Park show next year after all. Sue had been toying with an idea loosely based around the Ornamental Kitchen Garden for this show, but vegetables are so much more difficult than flowers to get perfect at the right time that they decided to take two years over this project, to give Dave time to experiment with the skills of getting his vegetables to perform on cue. The next step after Tatton Park would be to do

one or maybe two Westminster shows, with the ultimate aim of getting to Chelsea, so it seemed that the forecast I made earlier in the year might prove to be correct. I hope so: an accolade of any sort from Chelsea would be a tremendous boost for the gardens.

~

In early September Les Dawson and Roy Barraclough came into the shop from one of the coaches. Of course it wasn't actually Les Dawson and Roy Barraclough; it was two lovely elderly ladies whose repartee was just like Cissy and Ada's.

Nick was doing a relief turn behind the counter in the shop when the first lady said, 'So what happened to Geoff Hamilton, then?' then shouted across to her friend, who had wandered to the other side of the shop, 'I'm asking what happened to Geoff Hamilton.'

Her friend juggled her false teeth into place, hitched up her bosom and nodded sagely.

'Well,' said Nick, 'in what context exactly?'

'Well, one minute he was there on telly and next minute he was gone,' after which she shouted across the shop, 'I said one minute he was there and next minute he was gone.'

Another juggle of the teeth, hitching of the bosom and a mumbled, 'Yes.'

Seed is carefully collected each year and stored in paper bags, ready for sowing in the following spring

A fine crop of onions is hung up to dry in the greenhouse

'Well,' said Nick, 'he died in 1996.'

'Oh dear', and another shouted comment: 'He says he died in 1996.'

Juggle and hitch and a mumbled, 'Oh, that's sad', followed by a shouted, 'We wondered, didn't we, we wondered.'

'How did he die, then?' said the first lady.

Nick was sorely tempted to say that Geoff fell off his bike, but he restrained himself and gave a polite explanation. At this there was a final shouted exchange and off they went – without buying anything. Never a dull moment with the great British public.

A more moving incident happened with another group of visitors shortly afterwards. Catherine, Peter, Sam and Sarah Barrett, who had travelled from Beccles in Suffolk, approached Sue in the coffee shop, bubbling with excitement and enthusiasm. They said that watching Geoff's *Cottage Gardens* series had completely changed their lives. They weren't gardeners at all at the time, but the series had inspired them to great things. They were so taken by it that they turned their front garden into an Artisan's Cottage Garden – an exact replica of the one Geoff built at Barnsdale. They said that they felt compelled to come to see the original, to see how well they'd done it. And they felt they'd done a really good job. They stopped to make an appreciative entry in the visitors' book, promised to return and were clearly uplifted by the whole Barnsdale experience. How Geoff would have loved that.

~

Sue was now completing the voice-overs for the new video. Initially she found this a bit daunting, as you would expect, but she soon got into the swing of it. Her biggest difficulty was to articulate the words 'Bacillus thuringiensis', which is hardly surprising. Try saying them quickly and you'll see what a tongue-twister they are. I know from my own experience that it is mighty difficult to sit in a room, all on your own except for sound engineers peering at you through a window, reading a pre-prepared script and trying to make it sound natural.

Then Nick and Sue set off on a quest for sponsorship for the video. This was uncharted territory for them, as they had never before sought sponsorship for anything bigger than a walk for the school. Their first port of call was Adam Pasco, an old and trusted friend, who is the editor of *BBC Gardeners' World Magazine*. He gave them good advice and they left him feeling confident that they could present their case well, although how successful they would be remained to be seen. Several sponsors had expressed a keen interest in being featured on the video, but none seemed to have wanted to talk about money – yet.

Having spent some £30,000 and put in a lot of hard work on the video, they either needed to sell a lot of videos or get a fair bit of sponsorship. These are the kind of worries that cause strong men to weep, but Nick and Sue seemed to be very laid back and confident that it would be successful. I just hoped Nick hadn't inherited Geoff's 'something will turn up' attitude. Something always did turn up for Geoff, of course, but his relaxed style didn't serve him well in his early career – though in the end it was the very thing that made him successful. On his record so far, however, I was sure Nick knew what he was doing.

Adam Pasco said he would feature the video in the December edition of *BBC Gardeners' World Magazine* as one of his regular 'bargain basement' offers, and Nick was thinking of including a copy of the very popular Barnsdale calendar with it. Sounded like a good idea to me. They also planned to try to sell it not only at Barnsdale but also at outlets like W.H. Smith, as well as other gardens and garden centres. I thought this could be an uphill struggle. Buyers at W.H. Smith were likely to be a very hard-nosed bunch and I had a feeling that they would ask for a very big mark-up and then buy a very small volume so that they could trial it in a few stores, just to see how it went. But Nick's young and resilient. A tough introduction to the cut-throat business of retail sales would do him no harm and he might even be much more successful than he dreamed. I hoped so. Nick had had many, many enquiries asking for a video about the gardens so he was hopeful that it would be successful.

The team were also turning their attention now to the programme of talks and demonstrations to be held in the new coffee-shop extension. Dave, as proud as punch of his huge family of vegetables, was described by Nick as 'like a greyhound in the trap ready to go' so that, like a mother on Parents' Day, he could show off his beautiful offspring to an admiring world. He had already prepared a talk and, with refreshing enthusiasm, knew exactly what he wanted to do. Adam Frost had been approached to do a talk about garden design, which with his abundant skills should be fascinating – certainly not one I wanted to miss. Geoff, of course, left a treasure-trove of names and addresses of interesting and knowledgeable people, so there were plenty of contacts to go at; although usually if they're good they're busy, so it was not going to be an easy task.

Nick and Sue were also trying to devise a way to amuse and interest the children who come to the gardens with their parents. Clearly bouncy castles and swings and slides would not be fitting, so they were trying to create a series of projects the kids could get involved in while their parents were being thoroughly boring and looking at plants and garden designs – doing the things they came for, in fact. Nick and Sue wanted to stimulate the beginnings of an interest in gardening, so the idea was to write a kind of project manual which would get the children involved in fun activities like looking for particular plants in particular gardens, searching for statues or other ornaments in the gardens, colouring pictures of flowers and vegetables, and so on. They also planned to build a children's garden, which would contain a swing and a sandpit. Much to Nick's disappointment he was unable to make it much more adventurous because of the health and safety regulations governing an open garden. The H&S inspectors are now so paranoid about kids falling off swings or finding wild-animal droppings in the sandpit that great care would have to be taken to avoid these so-called hazards. How we ever survived before there were all these regulations I will never know.

~

Everyone was delighted by the arrival of two Japanese students, Ikuko and Tatsura, in their sandwich-year from Writtle. Ikuko's arrival at her interview with Sue for a student position in the nursery was a bit of a surprise. It's unusual to meet Japanese people in horticulture at the best of times, but Ikuko was something special. She is very small, dignified and polite with a mischievous giggle that seems to spread sunshine wherever she goes. She was fifty-seven years old and had come over to do a three-year course, leaving her poor old husband at home in Tokyo. She used to be an English teacher in Japan, so her English is perfect.

Tatsura, a young man in his twenties, was soon nicknamed 'Tats' and fitted in admirably with the rest of the staff. He comes from Kashiwa City, just outside Tokyo (I had to get him to spell the name twice before I grasped it), and he had got a degree at Reading University under his belt before he even started his course at Writtle. His dream, he told me, was to become a landscape designer, like Adam Frost, and he was to be shared with Adam by Barnsdale, so he was to alternate between the two: he'd do one month at Barnsdale and one month with Adam, learning the landscaping business, before returning to Barnsdale.

Despite the great beauty of traditional Japanese gardens, both Ikuko and Tats told me that they were attracted to work in England because of their desire to work with the cottage-garden style, which is becoming more and more popular in Japan. Japanese gardens concentrate much more on design, foliage and form in their gardens and it seems that there is a great desire in Japan for the riot of colour that an English cottage garden can bring.

Ikuko's burning ambition was to translate Geoff's book on cottage gardens into Japanese and to get it published there. I thought she might have to do some hard bargaining with the British publishers, but she seemed very determined. The work she was doing at Barnsdale was her first experience of 'hands-on' horticultural work, which at the age of fifty-seven seemed a very courageous step, but she seemed to be enjoying herself hugely. It was a great pleasure to meet two such enthusiastic, determined and cheerful people.

Despite the fact that the Japanese do not use Latin names to identify plants, both Ikuko and Tats were learning them fast, which must have been very difficult for people for whom English is a second language and Latin a third. Their tutor at Writtle, Mike Able, taught Nick when he was there, so, just like the gardening business they are both in, there seems to be a wonderful continuity. Unfortunately neither of them were staying in the hall of residence dedicated to Geoff's memory, so that's as far as the coincidence went.

~

I met the two angelic Annes from Ashby in early September. Anne Spooner and Anne Warren were good friends, both living in Ashby-de-la-Zouch in Leicestershire. This was Anne Spooner's first visit to Barnsdale. She had just come back from a holiday in the Cotswolds, where she had visited Hidcote Manor and Barnsley House. Modesty forbids me to mention

Beautiful.
– Nancy Long, Jen Fladayer, Betty Bowens, Minnesota, USA

There must be a fabulous garden in heaven.
– Anne Griffiths, Solihull

that she said that she liked what she had seen at Barnsdale much better, but she did. She explained that this was because it was extremely well signposted, so visitors could easily find their way around, it had a lot of good ideas and most of the plants were clearly labelled. Like so many other visitors, she also liked the way the garden was divided into a lot of small gardens, which she could easily identify with and which closely represented the size of her own garden, making it easy to visualise how to transport ideas from one location to the other.

Cool!

– Toby (aged thirteen)

Anne Warren had visited before, just after Geoff had died, when the gardens were, as she put it, 'in limbo' – in other words in the very first stages of development. I explained how it had been necessary to change the gardens when Geoff died – maintaining them all at once instead of just small areas at a time, as Geoff did when their sole purpose had been to satisfy the requirements of *Gardeners' World*; and working to different planting requirements, which meant doing constant battle with the results of Geoff's tendency to grossly overplant because this looked better on television and cutting back or removing plants that were perfectly good but had just got too big for their boots. Anne could now see how much effort had been required to get the gardens into the state they were now in and she was very complimentary about the results.

Both Annes wanted to come back in the spring, to see the spring flowers, and again a little later to see roses in full bloom. The reason they had come in September was to see how autumn colour could be achieved. Like many other gardeners, they found that spring and summer flowers were abundant in their gardens but when autumn brought its chillier winds and rain they began to withdraw into their shells and look dull and uninteresting. One of the things they had learned from their visit was that this was not inevitable and they were now armed with lists of autumn-flowering plants and a determined glint in their eyes. I had a feeling that a small part of Ashby-de-la-Zouch would be brighter and more optimistic next autumn.

Anne Spooner's parting tale was about her son, who had avidly watched Geoff's programmes from the age of seven and was totally enthralled and inspired. When they moved into their new house in Ashby he drew a design for the garden and then helped enthusiastically to choose the plants and to get the garden built. Anne felt that this success was due to the fact that Geoff was neither too grand nor too technical, so young people could easily identify with him. Once Anne's son became a teenager the call of the wild was stronger than the call of the garden, but Anne was confident that he would get back to it before long. In any case, that was one young person Geoff inspired to get involved, which was one of his major objectives.

~

At the end of September, on the day after her opening night, Penelope Keith and her husband, true to their word, returned to Barnsdale to see the gardens in more detail. Glowing from a very successful opening, when she played to a full house, she spoke in very complimentary terms about their visit. They loved the gardens, they enjoyed their lunch and we expect to see them again at some time in the future.

After a lot of pacing the room and heart-searching, Sue finally completed the designs for next year's Gardeners' World Live. She came up with a garden based on a central Y-shaped grass path leading to a bench at the base of the Y, surrounded by trees. Outside the paths would be two huge borders filled with planting and in the middle an attractive urn surrounded by herbs and ground-cover plants.

In the ornamental gardens general maintenance went on as ever – cutting back herbaceous plants, giving the hedges their final haircut for the winter, dead-heading, lawn-mowing and so on.

At the Drought Garden at Rutland Water, planting had reached the second phase. This was the alpine planting, which added a lot of starry-eyed plants, giving a lift to the whole design. The entire area was mulched with recycled council waste, which is composted on a private farm near Peterborough. The farmer, seeing the writing on the wall for conventional farming, diversified into compost – an unlikely but highly enterprising sideline that grew to be big business. He collects all the green council waste and supplements it with waste from the street markets, all of which he piles up into huge heaps and periodically turns with a big mechanical bucket. He makes beautiful loam-like compost, saving millions of cubic feet of landfill space and doing his very big bit for the environment as well. I understand he makes a good profit into the bargain. Eventually his customers buy back their own waste, so he's recycling not only waste but money as well. Enterprising, or what? Good luck to him, I say. Nick was proposing to buy a lorryload for soil conditioning in the winter and had high hopes that it would be very successful. Good gardeners get very excited about their compost and Nick is no exception.

David, the nursery supervisor, left in October, having decided that he wanted to

The hard-fruit harvest was bounteous, with no hint of a pest or disease, even though they had not seen a sprayer since the trees were planted

'spend more time with his family'; certainly the job is hectic and demanding. He went to work in an excellent local nursery, where he could concentrate on growing rather than becoming involved with the customers. He would be good at that and we all wished him well.

But now a replacement had to be found, so Sue advertised and was lucky enough to attract a young lady called Elizabeth Clark. Also an ex-Writtle student, she had been working at Hyde Hall near Chelmsford, one of the RHS gardens, so her standards were clearly very high and her knowledge and experience as sound as a bell, though she was only twenty-two. Having a lively personality, she would be a tremendous asset as an advisor to the visitors to the nursery. She knew her plants inside out and had the character and patience to get the information across. She would obviously be of enormous value generally and particularly with the talks and demonstrations, which she had done before for the RHS. She was also an expert flower-arranger, so that would add another strength to Betty's arm when things got hectic.

As many impetuous young girls do, she had fallen for some lucky fellow and was to marry him. Her husband-to-be had a job in Peterborough, which was why she was moving to the area. She couldn't start until November, but her arrival was eagerly awaited.

Publicity went out for the first of next year's talks and demonstrations, which was to be on the subject of an introduction to organic gardening for new gardeners. It was to be held in February when, for a modest fee, visitors could listen to a talk on best practice, which would be followed by an opportunity to pursue the subject with the specialists over a good lunch. Then they would tour the gardens and see a demonstration of some of the more interesting aspects of the art. There would also be a question-and-answer session, designed to help visitors to solve any special problems they had in their own gardens. On the same day there would be two half-day sessions, one on soft-fruit pruning and care and the other on soft-fruit propagation.

This year Dave overcame his carrot jinx and produced some very fine specimens

Later in the spring a guided tour of the gardens was planned, followed by a 'gardeners' question time', which always seems to be popular with the visitors. These events would not only nurture Geoff's passion for inspiring people to garden in natural ways but also, for the business, bring in some much-needed cash during the long and worrying period when the gardens have very few visitors.

Another thing in the pipeline that could help provide a buffer against the thin months was the establishment of a garden-maintenance service. Visitors had continuously been asking whether such a service was available and, with all the expertise that had now accumulated at Barnsdale, it seemed an obvious next step. It would mean buying some new equipment and transport, as well as taking on more staff, so a careful business plan had to be constructed. When the gardens were in full swing and maintenance at Barnsdale at its height the extra staff could also be used profitably back home, so the risks seemed low. However, this did not stop cautious Nick planning and preparing with the utmost care. I often wonder how the son could be so unlike the father – whereas Geoff was extravagant and optimistic Nick always thinks carefully, searching out the pitfalls and problems before he makes his move. Geoff would have jumped in with both feet, knowing that 'it will be all right on the night'.

~

October, of course, is the season for the fruit and vegetable harvest, which seemed to have been pretty good at Barnsdale this year. In fact Nick told me that he was reeling from the quality of Dave's carrots. You will remember that Dave wakes up screaming in the night from the burden of guilt he constantly carries from his inability to grow good carrots, but this year has been different and the burden seems to have been lifted. Despite a continuing battle against slugs and some casualties, he produced a prolific crop which were long, straight and free from carrot fly – and Dave was a new man. His normally smiling face became positively angelic and he walked his plot in a state of euphoria. It's wonderful what a good carrot will do for a man.

The potato harvest was excellent, the tubers largely free from damage from slugs and wireworm; and the hard fruit was abundant. Only about half the potential apple crop had been harvested, however, because the visitors, who obviously enjoy a crisp, sweet apple as they walk round, helpfully harvest the other half. The only

protection from this is provided by the apple arch, which obligingly suffers from scab every year. This is another example of Geoff accommodating the needs of the BBC. He sited the arch in a spot which is really too damp and sunless for apples but provided an ideal opening shot for the approach of a camera into the main garden. Now that the surrounding trees and shrubs have grown prolifically there is too little air circulation to ensure a scab-free crop, especially in a damp year. But because of the scab, the visitors tend to avoid the apples, in the erroneous belief that it may affect the taste or their digestion. It is noticeable that in the rest of the gardens, where the fruit has been planted in more amenable positions, there has hardly been any scab at all. The apple arch is one of the few times when Geoff departed from his normal mantra that position and soil type are the most important factors in any planting programme – but with the heavies of the mighty BBC at his back it was his only option.

The tops of the carrots are removed before plunging into pots of sand for winter storage

Root crops like carrots are stored in sharp sand, on end in pots, so that they are readily available for use during the winter, while the bigger roots, like celeriac (which is harvested later in the year), are stored in bark. They then all go down to the wonderful Victorian cold store at Exton Nurseries, where they take their place among apples and pears, stored in plastic freezer bags, and potatoes, in paper sacks, which also have a winter berth there. There is a deep sense of security and well-being about knowing that all these provisions are stored safely away – and the luxury of the smell in that store has to be experienced to be believed.

Dave dug his potatoes this year by the light of the full moon – at least, a nearly full moon: the celestial powers had the bad grace to cause it to rain on the night of the full moon, making digging impossible. Dave was as earnest as could be about his belief that this was when it should be done. Nick accepts the Druid's practice, although he has firmly drawn the line at dancing naked among the visitors. That would certainly frighten the horses. Dave's beliefs stem from pagan times, when there were set times to deal with the cultivation of all crops. For example, there were seed days, leaf days, root days and fruit days each month, when pagan ritual demanded that the ground should be tilled, seed should be sown, weeds should be pulled and harvesting should take place. Dave theorises that there is some ancient science behind this. He argues, for example, that roots should be dug either at full moon or new moon because between these there is most likely to be rain, so the harvest is easier and the roots cleaner. I'm not at all sure there are any meteorological data to support this theory, but there is no doubting the strength of Dave's belief. He buys a calendar every year that tells him which are the most favourable days for each cultivation activity for each type of crop, and that forms the basis his programme of work for the year. Sceptical though some of the staff are about Dave's belief, there are certainly two useful spin-offs from it: there is no doubt that it fills Dave with a powerful enthusiasm for his work and gives him a disciplined framework to work to; and Nick gets some free overtime that he could only get from a Druid.

~

One day in October Nick was concerned to be approached by a visitor who drew his attention to a very scathing comment that had appeared in the visitors' book. As he takes all complaints seriously, he hurried over to the coffee shop and found that it was one of the comments that appear three or four times a year: that the gardens look untidy and that all the plants have been allowed to grow into one another, creating a poor memorial to Geoff – the sort of comment that, as I have explained, Nick believes fails to appreciate what kind of garden Geoff was trying to

OK. Some plants dead.

– Andrew Booth, Hants

create. Nick was heartened to notice that directly under the comment somebody else had written, 'Well, they're obviously not gardeners!' He read down a little further and found that all subsequent comments were effusive with praise, until he came upon one from 'Polska'. The problem here was that it had been written in Polish, so Nick thought that he would have to wait until another Pole visited before he knew whether it was good or bad and whether any action was required.

But, as luck would have it, when he walked over to the shop the Polish authors of the comment were in there. They had come over to visit a Polish cousin who lived in Leicester, who spoke good English and explained that they had written that Barnsdale was fabulous, and even better than it had looked on television. It turned out that *Gardeners' World* was received in Poland and they were avid fans, so when they discovered that Barnsdale was close to Leicester they just had to visit. Geoff seemed to be still selling his wares, even five years after his death.

Now that the video was complete, notices had been displayed about its forthcoming release and there was a lot of interest from the visitors to the gardens – in fact about fifty per cent said that they would like to buy a copy. More exciting still was the fact that quite a few retailers had expressed an interest – W.H. Smith, Sainsbury's, Debenham's, Littlewoods, Co-Op, Woolworth's, John Lewis and a number of other major outlets, including the HDRA and the RHS. It would be trite to say that everything was coming up roses, but the signs were certainly looking good. Nick cannily priced the video at £9.99 because it's what he called a 'one-note payment', which, he was told by the retail trade, is a great incentive for people to buy. To me it's just money, but then I don't belong to today's merry band of obsessive shoppers.

~

By mid-October the gardens were still looking surprisingly resplendent with colour and bright foliage.

One of my favourite gardens at this time of the year is the Plantsman's Garden, which is devoted much more to plants than to hard-landscaping. It is designed to make Geoff's point that while hard-landscaping can add a great deal to a garden design it is often overdone and the real skill comes with the choice, position and maintenance of the plants; and to demonstrate how effective a good planting plan can be.

Now, in a kind of gentle harmony, it had peonies still in flower, sedums showing off their wonderful foliage with deep-red florets just beginning to make their presence felt, *Euonymus fortunei* 'Emerald Gaiety', which is an evergreen foliage plant with white-edged, deep-green leaves, and the ever-popular *Penstemon* 'Geoff Hamilton'.

The newly emerging, bright-red leaves of photinias, contrasting with the glossy green of the older leaves, sat alongside clumps of *Geranium clarkei* x *collinum* 'Kashmir

LEFT *Heuchera* 'Chocolate Ruffles' shows off its finery in the Plantsman's Garden
RIGHT The Plantsman's Garden is an inspiration for gardeners wishing to find new and unusual plants to beautify their gardens

White', still bearing loose clusters of white, cup-shaped flowers, and one of my favourite plants, rudbeckia, with large, daisy-like, brilliant-yellow flowers. In the middle of the superb brick paths which dissect the garden is a circular bed filled with a wide variety of plants, among them echinacea, an upright plant with large, daisy-like flowers in summer, *Taxus baccata* 'Fastigiata', standing proud in the middle, *Linum perrene*, which bears delicate, pure-blue flowers on slender stems in summer, an *Acer palmatum* 'Kashima' with its deeply divided leaves just turning a brilliant red and some stately grasses to finish the picture. For anybody wishing to see some unusual plants exquisitely blended together, this is certainly the place to come.

As one walks from the coffee-shop door, which is the entrance to the gardens, there is a handsome greeting and promise of good things to come in the form of a huge herbaceous border. This was still aflame with achillea, almost assaulting the eye with its mass of golden

bloom. A great expanse of deep-violet Michaelmas daisies stood next to it, offset by a pale-yellow potentilla with flattish, saucer-shaped flowers. The graceful blue buddleja still had a few butterflies feasting from its nectar and there was a suspicion of the gentle rustling of a foraging hedgehog. Close by in the grass bed, which looks good all the year with a great variety of grasses of all shapes, colours and sizes, the narrow leaves of a stand of miscanthus – stately bamboos – were just turning bronze.

In the Elizabethan Garden many of the crops had been harvested by now, but there were still some mouth-watering Brussels sprouts, kale, lettuce, beetroot and even some late courgettes, spring onions, crimson-flowered broad beans and peas. Dave would cover these vulnerable crops with cloches shortly, to avoid damage from rain and frost, in an attempt to

ABOVE Dave's curly Kale is a fine ornamental plant as well as the provider of delicious meals
OPPOSITE Skilful work on the topiary in the Reclaim Garden has resulted in some exquisitely shaped pyramids

extend the season for as long as he could. A very attractive touch here is the little clump of wild strawberries planted at the corners of each bed, as well as edging the circular herb garden that stands in the centre of the garden.

Strolling through this lovely little garden you will chance upon another tiny herb garden, designed by Robin Williams for *Gardeners' World.* It is laid out as the corner of a bigger garden and as well as the beds there is a fascinating array of terracotta pipes of various heights and sizes, each containing its own herb. This is a very inventive way to prevent the more vigorous herbs from overpowering the delicate specimens and to control the rapacious spread of plants like mint, which, without some containment, will take over your garden before you know it's happened.

The Country Garden was luminous with autumn-flowering plants, all still acting as benevolent hosts to butterflies, bees and insects of all descriptions. A glorious stand of Michaelmas daisies was simply covered with butterflies all getting their fast food while the going was good. A small pond in one corner accommodated water boatmen, figure-skating as though they were in an Olympic final, small birds nervously drinking, one eye always looking for the approach of predators, and a supercilious toad, whose face I could just see as he peered out smugly from his home in some foliage close by, probably thinking 'Poop poop', as toads do. The small pergola which you pass through on your way out of this garden was covered in abundantly flowering clematis and a climbing rose, smothered in bright-red and golden hips.

A little further on is the Courtyard Garden, designed to show what can be done with a very small area where grass is not a practical possibility. This plot is divided into four individual courtyards, each one designed by Adam Frost to demonstrate a different but inexpensive idea. The first is a small circular patio, approached by a path of stone paving edged with patterned bricks and contrasted with some box topiary cleverly cut into neat spirals. Box hedges, also neatly clipped, surround the beds which fill the rest of this tiny garden and a bold yew hedge forms a dense background which would exclude all sound of traffic or noisy neighbours. Next is a small patio which, unlike its neighbour, is delightfully curved and made from pebbles set into an intricate design and edged with cobblestones. Here there are no borders but a number of tubs and containers, filled with yellow cascades of nasturtiums and fuchsias, still showing a bright light from their hanging lanterns, all offset by the soft-grey foliage of the helichrysum – ideal for an elderly or disabled person.

In the other corner is another paved courtyard, this one with a small greenhouse in the corner and shrub borders planted with *Carex hachijoensis* 'Evergold', a tuft-forming, evergreen perennial sedge with narrow yellow-striped leaves, campanulas which bear delicate bell-shaped flowers throughout the spring and summer, a mass of tall, elegant grasses, hemerocallis, the sweet-scented day lily, so called because the radiant yellow flowers last only for one or, if you're lucky, two days, and many others, cleverly arranged to give some colour and foliage all the year round.

A quite formal courtyard stands opposite, designed with straight, gravelled paths skirting a rectangular pond with raised, paved stepping stones marching across, towards a delightful wooden arbour, made by Peter Wallace of Woodworks in Uppingham, who was a great, long-time friend of Geoff's. The formality of the garden is softened by borders planted with roses, penstemons which were still showing some flower, peonies and other plants, again planted with a continuity of interest in mind.

The Town Paradise Garden was still presenting itself as a fitting tribute to Geoff's finest programme, which was being repeated by the BBC. You enter it through a conservatory and, crossing a patio, are led by one of the paths to a splendid gazebo, again built by Peter Wallace, and decorated with some enchanting wood carving executed by Glynn Mould from Oundle in Northamptonshire. The gazebo sits invitingly by a pond, which is planted with bulrushes, water lilies and many marginal plants and is apparently fed from a lion's-head

Good ideas. Brought back memories of Geoff. They don't make programmes like he made anymore.

– M. G. Yallop, Morayshire, Scotland

ABOVE The small herb garden, with each plant cleverly contained in a tubular container, makes a unique design feature and a convenient growing method for the small garden or patio OPPOSITE The neatly clipped box hedges form the perfect partner for the formality of the paving in the Country Garden

feature (the water is actually pumped), which spills water into a tinkling rill. The effect is not only sensational but also deeply calming and restful. My eye was drawn to a magnificent *Leucanthemella serotina,* which was a giant cloud of huge, daisy-like white flowers. Close by were roses still blooming strongly in the warm autumn breeze, together with *Schizostylis coccinea* 'Major', the Kaffir lily, which bears spikes of cup-shaped pink flowers, while aconitums mingled comfortably with tender perennials such as argyranthemums and osteospermums, all combining to give the relaxing gardener the best kind of companionship available. Just the place for the evening gin and tonic.

CHAPTER SIX

~

Winter Begins
its
Advance

~

November and December

Winter Begins
its Advance

~ November and December

A superb October ended on a high note of sunshine and warmth which went on into first week of November. This long spell of warm weather – the warmest October since records began, no doubt caused by the global warming that Geoff warned about so often – resulted in some extraordinary events. At Barnsdale almost all the trees were still fully in leaf, the air was full of birdsong and bees and butterflies were still feeding enthusiastically.

This warmth was part of a continuing trend that is good news for some animals and plants but ominous for others. Insects will certainly thrive, including the pestilential ones such as aphids and thrips which will continue to ravage plants, unless we have some good old-fashioned frosts during the winter. But some migratory birds, we are told, have become confused by the warm weather and instead of leaving for foreign lands stay put, missing their flight like tardy passengers at Heathrow; others are being driven further and further north. While insectivorous birds will find plenty to eat, it seems likely that we shall end up with as large a population of birds but with far less variety. Already we are losing bird species at a rate of knots, not only because of climate change but also because of intensive agricultural practices.

ABOVE The tough, thorny berberis will survive even the hardest winters

But the good news is that gardens are becoming the new favoured habitat and playing a much more important part in the preservation of some fragile species, even in intensely urban areas. Barnsdale is a fine example of what can be done to encourage them. What was once just a relatively uninteresting piece of flat grassland is now buzzing, humming, twittering, snuffling with (and, regrettably, sometimes suffering from) a huge population of birds, insects, reptiles and small mammals. So the message from Chairman Geoff would be, I'm sure, fill your gardens with trees, shrubs, flowering plants and, yes, even weeds, so that we can combat the depredations of intensive agriculture and chemicals and preserve our heritage before it is changed for ever.

The thing that doesn't change, however, is the certain and secure knowledge that the whole cycle will soon begin again. With the garden now closed to all but season-ticket holders and the high-season maintenance jobs at an end, the staff could now devote their time to preparations for next year, to ensure that it was even more dazzling than last. All the tender perennials were being lifted, potted up where necessary and moved into their snug winter quarters in greenhouses or tunnels. Those tender plants

> *Amazing amount of colour on a beautiful November day.* – Alan and Pam Philip, Ashbourne, Derbyshire

that had to remain in place, the bay trees and the tree ferns, were swathed in warm layers of horticultural fleece. Hardy plants that had outgrown their space were now lifted and divided and the space filled with a small, more respectable-sized portion of the plant. The remainder of these plants were passed over to the nursery, where they would be further divided and potted up for sale next year.

The peaches and apricots in the Ornamental Kitchen Garden were also covered with fleece, not because they are not frost hardy but because of the danger of frost damaging the blossom in the spring. It was obviously not imperative that they were covered at this time of the year, but cautious Nick didn't want them to get forgotten. When the fleece is out, he said, let's do the whole job so that we can forget about it. That comfortable cover would stay in place until May, or even June, although it would be rolled back during sunny and warm days and replaced at night.

Even the pumps in the many water features were removed so that there would be no risk of damage by frost. They were cleaned, serviced and stored, ready for work as soon as the gardens opened fully again in March.

There is no opportunity to do what most good amateur gardeners do to prepare their greenhouses or tunnels for the winter – clean and disinfect them; there simply isn't enough time in the day to clear everything out, disinfect and put it all back again. But all pots and trays are washed, the staging is thoroughly cleaned and the capillary matting is renewed each year. Otherwise the staff just have to trust to a rigid regime of hygiene and tidiness to ensure that there is no significant build-up of disease.

Vigilance also plays a very big part in pest and disease control at Barnsdale. If you are sharp-eyed enough to see the beginnings of an outbreak before it has taken serious hold, it can be easily controlled – usually just by nipping off some leaves or even throwing out one or two pots with infestations of pests. I have never forgotten Geoff telling me about an old organic gardener he had once met who had as clean a garden as you could wish to see. When Geoff asked him what he did to achieve such immaculate pest control he just smiled and said, 'I look a lot!' So far Sue, whose special responsibility is the nursery, has found that these methods have worked well; and, when you consider that the nursery has been operating for nearly twelve years, it can't be bad practice.

Wonderful. Good to see an odd weed or failure; it makes it perfect. – Lionel and Kathy Peak, Feckenham, Worcs

Some perennial and alpine seeds had been sown and were already germinating, starting the process of renewal and regeneration – the thought of which always fills me with optimism and excitement and which is one of the great gifts given to the gardener.

Sue took down all the wall pots and hanging baskets and planted them up with winter plants, trying to avoid the use of pansies, wallflowers and other traditional plants, so as to show winter visitors new ideas and, she hoped, to inspire them to do the same. This might create another tradition, which will go out of fashion again and we will return to wallflowers and pansies, but that remains to be seen.

A small but pleasing success was the result of the clear signposting and directing of visitors round prescribed routes. Not only did many visitors tell me that they found this very helpful, especially as there are so many small gardens on the site that the layout could easily be confusing, but also the grass stood the trials of the tramping feet much better, which meant that no replacement turfing would have to be done this year. Obviously this would be a significant saving in both time and money. Last year, which was wet but perhaps not *as* wet, half the garden had to be returfed because of excess wear.

The staff had to deal with the arrival of 620 bare-rooted rose plants, all of which had to be potted up and transported to Exton Nurseries to stand out until the busy season starts again. These had been bought from one of Geoff's great allies and friends, David Austin of David Austin Roses. It is pleasing for me to see that Nick and Sue still buy all their roses, for sale in the nursery, from the company. They do this not only for reasons of friendship, however: they buy from him for commercial reasons. It just happens that David is without doubt one of the best rose-growers in the country, so they know that whatever they get from him is going to be good. Two thirds of the roses that had been bought were the variety 'Geoff Hamilton', which bears a stunning pale-pink flower and has been David Austin's best-seller for several years now and is always much in demand at Barnsdale.

~

Advertising about the short courses that were to be run was beginning to show encouraging results. After just one mention in Amateur Gardening there was a clamour for places, which suggested they were going to be extremely popular. Sue, having seen advertisements for RHS

The staff relax for their tea-break in the cosy comfort of Dave's shed

ABOVE A dusting of frost will enhance the appearance of any evergreen plant RIGHT Visitors love to browse in the Nursery, choosing unusual plants to enhance their gardens

courses held at venues other than RHS gardens, phoned to tell them about the courses that were planned at Barnsdale. Shortly afterwards the RHS phoned back to say that they were anxious to have the opportunity to run some RHS courses at Barnsdale before anybody else did. There seemed to be a strong possibility that some of the courses – though not all, because Nick and Sue are determined that Barnsdale should become known for this kind of work in its own right – would be sponsored by and advertised by the mighty RHS. An accolade indeed, as well as a very effective marketing aid.

The video was selling well in advance of its release in November, so Nick and Sue had discussions with Steve Cowper, whose production company made it, to see if there was any possibility of getting television work out of it, or whether it would be suitable for 'in-filling' clips for other television programmes, in the hope of further mileage from the heavy investment that has gone into it so far, as well as some powerful advertising. We would have to sit tight and wait to see if either materialised.

A sign of the impending popularity of the video came when a chap rang the gardens and left a message on the answering machine. He said, 'Hello, hello. I'm just ringing to say that I've just ordered a copy of that video. You know, the one about Geoff's place. Just phoned to let you know. OK? Bye.' He left no name, no telephone number, no address. He was just so chuffed that he'd ordered it he felt he had to tell somebody. I have to say I warmed to him immensely. I just love people like that. No cynicism, no malice, just an innocent charm. I bet he was a wow with the ladies when he was a lad.

By mid-November the video had begun to sell in volume – about fifty to sixty enquiries were being received every day. At this rate it should easily cover its cost and begin to make a profit fairly soon. I asked Nick and Sue whether or not they had felt any misgivings about treading in Geoff's footsteps, because he was, after all, a consummate professional and a very hard act to follow. I have to admit that I am conscious of him every time I do a radio or television interview, or even a piece for a newspaper, because I feel that I will never be able to match his standard. But both Nick and Sue stoutly maintained that the thought never crossed their minds. The

Came in snow.
Will come again.

– Margaret Dakin, Ipswich

video, they explained, was not supposed to be set in Geoff's image, and neither was it instructional, as Geoff's work was. Its purpose was to show a little of what happens in the gardens now that they are no longer Geoff's domain, how they have changed and what goes on behind the scenes.

~

Now was the time of the year to take stock and review. Looking at arrangements for next year, Nick and Sue decided to make a change in the winter visiting hours, which should benefit visitors considerably. Season-ticket holders had always been able to come into the gardens at any time of the year, but the next year the gates would be open to other visitors every day from November to February, from 10.00 a.m. to 4.00 p.m.; and, although the coffee shop would not be open for meals, if anybody was hardy enough to visit in the depths of winter they would certainly be welcome to a hot drink – and there are unquestionably some very hardy souls about. In the second week in November, when the weather changed dramatically with a freezing Arctic wind and flurries of snow driving everybody indoors, an elderly couple turned up, she clad in open-toed sandals and aided by a stick, and they toured the gardens for a couple of hours, thoroughly enjoying themselves. Next stop, Everest.

It is good to visit the gardens at either end of the winter because in November there is still a lot of colour and interest and in February the bulbs begin to appear – and they are well worth seeing. Many a garden is lovely during the summer but fades into insignificance as soon as winter arrives, and Barnsdale gives people a good idea of what to plant for winter and spring colour to brighten up the garden. Nick and Sue also decided to open on Boxing Day and New Year's Day so that people could fill that difficult time when the excitement is over and they have to think what to do with the relatives. So if you have a yearning to see a bleary-eyed and hung-over Nick, you know the time to visit.

Additionally, during the winter weekends the entrance fee would be reduced on the grounds that not only is there less to see at that time of the year but also visitors may be excluded from parts of the gardens because work is going on there. Also, as all the water features are turned off, the visual effect is to some extent reduced.

From 1 March 2002 the gates would open at 9.00 each morning, rather than 10.00, and close at 5.00 p.m., but in June, July and August they would close at 7.00 p.m, rather than 5.00, so that visitors can enjoy the intoxicating beauty of the late-evening sunshine and the extraordinary tranquillity of the stillness of such fragrant air.

OPPOSITE Even in the midst of winter grasses make a dramatic and mysterious statement INSET Jon frequently visits the Drought Garden for general maintenance and to replace plants that are past their best

~

The enterprise of Nick and Sue seems to know no bounds. Their latest idea was to obtain a licence to hold weddings at Barnsdale. They would not be equipped to hold the reception there, but what an idyllic setting it would be for the civil ceremony – and there is an excellent hotel at the end of the avenue that could easily handle the reception. The ceremony would probably be held either in one of the arbours, if the weather was fine, or in the conservatory attached to the Paradise Garden if not. A marquee-type temporary building would be erected outside the doors of the conservatory to accommodate the guests and the whole of the gardens would then be available for photographs. That would seem to be a rather better arrangement than the nondescript yards or gardens attached to most register offices and the idea may well attract a lot of people.

Certainly the registrar who came to look at the suitability of the gardens for this type of event was highly enthusiastic and said he would support the application without demur. Mind you, first there was a lot of work to be done. Fire officers would have to approve, policemen had to visit and a licence to sell alcohol had to be obtained, which in itself would be a great advantage because for regular visitors a glass of wine could then be served with meals. Nick and Sue only proposed to sell small bottles of wine, but nevertheless they would have to go on some kind of publicans' course in order to get the licence. Seems odd to have to do all that for the privilege of handing over small bottles of wine in the coffee shop, but if it has to be done they will do it. It'll be nice to have a publican in the family.

Meanwhile the garden-maintenance service was launched and within only two or three weeks had a steady stream of enquiries and a few firm bookings. It meant that Jon would have another responsibility on his plate, but he seemed to be looking forward to the challenge. He would make a start using the people the gardens already employed, but it looked likely that more would have to be recruited if orders flowed in. Fortunately there was a sufficient stock of machinery and equipment already available at Barnsdale so it seemed that, initially at any rate, the only capital expenditure that would be needed would be for a vehicle of some kind to carry the staff to and from each job.

Cleaning and maintenance of the machinery is a vital winter job, which will avoid breakdowns in the hectic summer months

This service would also take some careful planning and co-ordination, so Jon would need all his administrative wits about him as well. But he'd cope. He always does.

Early November saw the arrival of Elizabeth, the newly appointed nursery supervisor. She was now Elizabeth Barrett, having married just a few weeks before. (In fact I may be making an unwelcome disclosure to her husband when I reveal that she had some difficulty remembering her new name when I asked her.) She is a most engaging, lively person (who likes to be known as Tizzy), with lots of energy and good ideas, so she seemed to be just what the doctor ordered. When she arrived the seed-sowing and propagation were already in full swing, so she was a busy body from the start.

The RHS telephoned at the end of November, following up the interest they had expressed in mounting some courses at Barnsdale, and booked the first two. The following autumn, Dave would present a course on growing unusual fruit and vegetables and their use in the kitchen, and Nick would present a course and demonstration on propagation of plants from soft and hardwood cuttings. These courses would open up a whole new educational facet of the work at Barnsdale and both Nick and Sue were excited about the prospect. I may come to sit at the back and heckle, just see what they're made of – but on second thoughts they may just be a match for me.

Farewell, Geoff. V. good.

– Pam and John Edwards, Nottingham

Work on the new souvenir guide was now begun in earnest. This time it was to be accompanied by a supplement showing each garden in detail, with designs and planting plans, so that anybody who wishes to use a Barnsdale garden as the basis for a design in their own garden can easily do so. The many people who loved Geoff and come to Barnsdale more as a pilgrimage than a visit will, I feel, be delighted to be able to take back a bit of his innovative spirit and his flare so that they can recreate it for themselves. The planting plans presented some problems because of the ever-changing nature of the gardens. Plants die or grow too large and some are replaced simply because there is something more appropriate to fill the space. Additionally, as I have explained, Nick doesn't know the names of all the plants. So it was decided that the plant list would identify the major plants and those that are unlikely to change. It should still provide a very useful guide to the plants – and all of them will, of course, be available in the nursery sales area.

~

By late November the stream of enquiries for the garden-maintenance service had turned into a torrent and Nick had to advertise for an additional member of staff. With the gardens now being visited only by a few hardy regulars it was indeed proving to be a way of providing a good back-up to tide the business over the seasonally sticky patch and keep the bank manager happy. This new flow of income would be augmented by sales of the video, which, only a couple of weeks after its launch, was selling about sixty copies a week. Not bad for a first attempt.

Interviews for a new member of staff to augment the garden-maintenance team took place at the end of December. Nick planned to get the new appointee working in the gardens first, under Jon's supervision, so that he could be absolutely sure that his work was good enough to launch upon an unsuspecting public. It would be a disaster for the reputation of the gardens for poor-quality work to be allowed, so a period of training was essential.

At the moment Ben and Tats were doing all the maintenance work but it would not be acceptable to keep them at it on a full-time basis. Ben, who initially joined earlier in the year on trial and was now a fully fledged member of the permanent staff, had proved to be a skilled, hard-working lad with tremendous enthusiasm, so it would only be fair to allow him to rotate around the available jobs as much as possible so that he could get sufficient experience to take his career a stage further. Tats, a highly trained, passionate gardener with the intelligence to go a long way in the business, was certainly not going to be satisfied with cutting grass and trimming hedges all day. So whoever was

Mahonia media 'Winter Sun' in its superb purple robes, sits like a lord in the Winter Border

employed on the maintenance side would always rotate from job to job, sometimes inside and sometimes outside, to give them as much experience in as wide a range of activities as possible. The final objective, strange though it may sound, is for the young 'improvers', as they used to be called when I was a boy, to leave Barnsdale with either a better job, a place at college or a determination to set up in competition. It is hoped that the senior people like Jon, the head gardener, Elizabeth, the nursery supervisor, and Dave, the vegetable supremo, will stay to advance within the business; but if they do there is a limit to the job prospects for the younger people, so they will be encouraged to learn as much as they can and then helped to move on if they want to.

~

The last few months of the year saw a few trials and tribulations. There had been one or two lovely and helpful people who had been obliged to leave this year but it was a particularly sad time for all the staff when Joan, who worked in the nursery and who was tremendously popular, was obliged to leave. Her husband became a victim of the tightening economic squeeze and was made redundant, so they decided to move back to Devon where their family lives. There was a subdued little presentation ceremony in the shop and I fancy I saw a tear here and there. Mind you, Nick always was a terrible blubber, just like his father. But she was wished Godspeed and showered with gifts before she sadly went her way.

Disaster struck just before Christmas when, as if to remind everybody that things could go badly as well as smoothly, a huge Pied Piper-led army of rats broke into the vegetable store at Exton Nurseries and ate practically everything. They had the good grace to leave a few parsnips, carrots, swedes, celeriac and beetroot, but they devoured all the potatoes like starving prisoners being offered their last meal. They ignored the rat poison they had been offered as an hors d'oeuvre and simply gorged themselves on a whole winter's supply of victuals for the troops. There was nothing for it but to shrug it off and call in the pest controller – and give the local supermarkets a little more business than they had expected that winter.

Rather predictably, the planning application for permission for a licence to stage weddings at Barnsdale was opposed by Exton Parish Council – on the grounds that too much traffic would be using the approach road. Nick was enraged at this, not only because, without exception, the Parish Council have opposed *every* planning application ever submitted, but also because they seemed to be unable to act in the interests of their residents. There is no doubt that this would provide more income and more opportunities for local businesses. Nobody had visited or telephoned Barnsdale to discuss the likely impact but they still saw fit to oppose the plan. Personally I have always been of the view that it is good sense not to fall out with your neighbours but to resolve differences by friendly negotiation, but clearly that view was not held by the Parish Council. Now if Nick had proposed a nuclear power station . . . But still, it was the County Council who would make the decision, so the battle was by no means lost.

But, despite such hiccups, which are an inevitable part of running an enterprise such as Barnsdale, the year drew to a close with some positive news. A letter arrived from the RHS to confirm that Barnsdale had been allotted a space at next year's Gardeners' World Live exhibition at the NEC in Birmingham. Allocation of space is by no means automatic, irrespective of your prominence or how many times you have exhibited before. Judgement is made largely on the basis of the quality of design that is submitted and the quality of previous designs, for which photographs have to be submitted, so this was quite a feather in the old cap.

The *BBC Gardeners' World Magazine* offer on the new video came to an end and was enormously successful. Four thousand copies were sold in all – far more than expected. A representative from Suttons Seeds came up to Barnsdale to meet Nick and Sue and as a result Suttons have agreed to sponsor the video, so the project looked set to be a winner. Nick and Sue were well pleased.

Sue, who had been visiting schools recently to demonstrate how to sow seeds and grow plants, raised this as a possible joint project with Suttons and was delighted to find that they had recently produced a special schools pack for supporting just this kind of venture. They agreed to send some packs to her so that she could use them for future demonstrations, which they believed should become a firm feature of the school curriculum. That could get a lot of kids started on a gardening future and, after the inevitable break while the requirements of their teenage hormones are satisfied, turn them into a new generation of gardeners.

On 21 December the gates closed and all the staff assembled at the Sun Inn at Cottesmore, a classy pub which serves the very best of victuals, for a very well-earned lunch on the governor. Despite a pretty disastrous start, with biting cold, torrents of rain and the foot-and-mouth epidemic keeping the visitors away earlier in the season, the year had turned out pretty well. Numbers were only slightly down on last year, the new shop and coffee shop were completed, the programme of talks and demonstrations had started, a new video had been made and was selling well and the garden-maintenance service looked very promising indeed. And, most importantly, thousands of people had enjoyed the gardens and had been inspired by all that they offer.

Now all that was needed was a good rest over Christmas (although Nick and Sue would still have to visit every day to water and check that all was well) to stoke up with optimism, ideas and enthusiasm for another great gardening year at Barnsdale.

Historical Note

When Geoff bought Barnsdale, where he was to spend the happiest and most fulfilling period of his adult life, it was a part of the estate of the Earl of Gainsborough, who had given the house and the land to his daughter Celestria Noel. The purchase of the house and land from Celestria Noel was negotiated with Viscount Campden, who manages the estate and is the son and heir of the Earl of Gainsborough. When Geoff moved in, the house was called the Grange; and he changed the name to Barnsdale to avoid confusing the millions of viewers who had watched his programme when it was broadcast from Barnsdale Hall, some half a mile up the road. The family owns, to this day, a large part of the nearby village of Exton and most of the surrounding land.

The history of the Earl of Gainsborough's estate is fascinating. The earliest reference I could find was of a deer park at Exton in 1185. Its boundary with Burley Park was in dispute early in the next century. The Harringtons were lords of the manor until 1613, when it was bought by Sir Baptiste Hicks, a wealthy wool merchant from Chipping Campden who had earlier become the first Viscount Campden. The Lord Harrington who inherited the Exton estate was very ambitious and tried to keep up with the lifestyle of the court of Queen Elizabeth I and the royal family and, in doing so, ran up enormous debts, which is why, in 1613, he was obliged to sell. Lord Harrington was also the guardian to the Queen of Bohemia, which explains the name of a ride down to the woods which is still called the Queen of Bohemia's Ride.

Viscount Campden's eldest daughter Juliana married Sir Edward Noel, another noble name in Leicestershire and Rutland. Viscount Campden bought the estate for his daughter. Sir Edward's father was Sir Andrew Noel, who came from Brooke, now a tiny village just outside Oakham. Sir Andrew, who was Sheriff of Rutland and an MP, was married to Mable Harrington, who was the sister of Lord Harrington; so, although the estate was owned by Viscount Campden, through his family it was still connected to the Harringtons. Sir Andrew, it is believed, was one of the favourite courtiers of Queen Elizabeth I.

In 1629 Viscount Campden died and Sir Edward Noel, who was already Lord Ridlington, also became the second Viscount Campden. In February 1661 Sir Edward Noel was created the Earl of Gainsborough by King Charles II, so his first title, Viscount Campden, became his secondary title and it passed to his son.

In the mid-nineteenth century a new entrance to the estate was made, featuring a magnificent pair of wrought-iron gates, resplendent with the family crest, flanked by a small gatehouse on either side and approached by a magnificent avenue of great trees. The avenue, which I believe to be one of the most dramatic and beautiful aspects of the Rutland countryside, was known by the hunting fraternity as 'the Dismal Mile' because of its supposedly gloomy appearance. I think they were totally misguided, but then I've always thought the hunting fraternity to be totally misguided. The original house had been damaged by fire in 1812 – badly enough for the family to have to move out into a Queen Anne house on the estate, which was now 'modified' and today forms the nucleus of the present house. The 'modification' quadrupled the size of the original Queen Anne house, so it must have been a very prosperous time for the family. The original house was then used as a place to teach carpentry to the boys of the village, but in 1914 it went up in flames again and was reduced to a complete ruin. The ruins still stand in the grounds, presumably as a reminder to the children that they shouldn't play with matches. Looking round the village today one can see some beautiful pieces of carved stonework adorning the stone cottages, which must have come from the ruins of the house. The ruins are now listed by English Heritage, so there will be no more snitching of the stonework in the future.

Before Geoff came to Barnsdale, it had always been farmed. A list of the assets of the Exton estate at the turn of the nineteenth century describes it thus:

Rent yearly, 6th April
Farm house and out offices
Cow house, hen house, calf place, all adjoining near, cowsheds, duck house, stable and
   granary, all adjoining near, forming three sides of the crew yard. Stone slated or tiled
Open wagon hovel near by, brick and tiled
Detached hovel, wood built and iron back of cowsheds
Water supply from rain supplied from Brook Farm for stock
For drinking purposes, deep well
Arable and pasture

The last farmers to live at Barnsdale, then known as the Grange, were Arthur and Betty Dalby. Arthur had succeeded his father and eventually his son took over the tenancy of the farm from his father, as was the custom in those days. It was only seventy acres but when Arthur Dalby was farming it, in the early 1950s and 60s, it was quite possible to make a living from a small acreage – which would be quite impossible today. It was a mixed farm in the very best sense of the word – with cows, sheep, pigs, laying hens, ducks and arable crops. It clearly did well, because in the early sixties he was able to buy Glebe Farm in Exton (which later became Highmead Farm) and the family moved out of the Grange, after which there was a succession of residential tenants, the land still being farmed by Arthur's son, also named Arthur. Arthur and Betty's daughter describes her childhood at the Grange as idyllic, spent playing in the spinney close to the house, collecting eggs, feeding calves and pigs and all the other magical things that farming children are able to do. It seems clear that there has been a long history of good husbandry and respect for the land at Barnsdale. Small wonder that Geoff was so happy there.

Index

Note: Page references in *italics* are to illustrations

Acknowledgements

I have been fortunate enough to receive the help and advice of a lot of people in the writing of this book and, if I thanked them all, it would take a sizeable supplement to do so. I will confine my thanks, therefore, to the principal players, but I hope that those people whom I have not been able to mention will understand that their contribution has been valued just as highly.

First, of course, I must thank Nick and Sue, for their patience and time in guiding me through the events at Barnsdale throughout the year, for checking all my facts and for allowing me unlimited access to their staff, who gave me an invaluable insight into their work. My thanks to each of them also.

Lynda, Geoff's wonderful wife, once more adopted her teacher's role and marked my work, correcting my grammar and putting many facts to rights. But, unlike my own school teachers, she added encouraging comments in red pen. For once I would have welcomed a detention.

Steve Hamilton, Geoff's eldest son, took all the pictures and I think the result is a testament to his skill. It was, as always, great fun to work with him and to bask in the pleasure of his zany sense of humour.

Celia Kent, my managing editor, was her usual unflappable self and she saw the whole thing through with quiet efficiency while regaling me with wonderful stories of singing in the chorus at the Proms, adventures in China, the splendour of her rooftop garden and many other things. Regrettably I was unable to prise from her any stories concerning the peccadilloes of other authors, but I shall keep trying.

I must also thank all the visitors who contributed to the book, most of whom I accosted unashamedly during their walks round Barnsdale and who submitted themselves indulgently to my questions with never a single objection or complaint. Nice people, gardeners.

I was lucky enough to be provided with one golden prize – the editor who worked with me on my last two books, Anne Askwith, who dazzles me with her uncanny ability to turn my clumsy prose into English and whose attention to detail is beyond compare. She was patient, encouraging and kind and I am most grateful to her.

Finally I must thank my ever-indulgent wife, who never grumbled at my long absences and interrupted my work only to provide a constant stream of victuals and good advice. She is, as ever, my strength and support.